Sue Cook's
Wonderful
CROSS STITCH
COLLECTION

Featuring hundreds of original designs

David & Charles

A DAVID & CHARLES BOOK

First published in the UK in 2000

ISBN 0 7153 0978 1

Photography by David Johnson
Book design by Kit Johnson
Printed in Italy by Milanostampa
for David & Charles
Brunel House   Newton Abbot   Devon

Contents

Introduction

This is my own 'rainy day book' and I hope it will become yours, too, whether to dip into for inspiration or just to pass an hour or so. When you flick through the pages you will find it is made up of hundreds of different charts, and there is something of me in every little design. I have grouped them under themes close to most stitchers' hearts, such as Home Thoughts, Gardening Pleasures and Childhood Days.

Each motif can be stitched on its own straight off the page to go in a card, or combined with others to make a sampler or other type of project. If you like the idea of designing your own original cross stitch, but are put off by the thought of drawing charts from scratch, use these designs as your starting point.

Throughout the book you'll find stitched examples of how the motifs can be combined, along with details of how these projects were made. You can either recreate these models exactly as they appear in the photographs or use them as a basis for your own ideas. I hope they will inspire you to create the unique design you want to stitch. Most of the designs are suitable for beginners, although some do take quite a lot of stitching. Most use only whole cross stitch, making them ideal for a wide range of fabrics.

I hope my Collection will become a useful addition to your cross stitch library that you return to on many occasions.

Many stitchers enjoy making cards and decorations for Christmas. These little angels can be stitched on perforated plastic for tree decorating. The motifs are charted on pages 118–20 and could be used for cards and other festive projects. To finish off a design stitched on perforated plastic, oversew the edges in a darker brown for contrast. Stick a piece of felt to neaten the back and stitch a folded length of ribbon securely to the top for hanging.

Designing a Sampler

I have three powerful computers to help me design, but they would be useless if I didn't also have my pencils and paper. Each of my designs, whether large or small, begins life as a sketch on graph paper. Many evolve from an idea that comes to me in the middle of the night. I love drawing and for me, a blank sheet of paper feels like the start of an adventure.

Now I know everyone does not share my enthusiasm for this part of the process. I also know that for many people a family celebration is the catalyst that awakes the designer within. To my way of thinking, when you rearrange motifs to suit your purpose and change some of the details and colours, you create a design that is uniquely yours, even if you didn't produce the original motif. By adding your creative input you are taking a first step from stitching to designing and you will find even greater pleasure in cross stitch as a result.

Do you want your design to reflect the hobbies and interests of a friend or family member? Perhaps your mum loves knitting or your dad likes DIY. You'll find motifs on these and many other themes in the book that would be ideal for a Mother's or Father's Day design. When you want to add names or dates to your sampler you can use the alphabets and numbers in the Special Days section or the large alphabet on page 126. You can also incorporate letters or numbers from other sources if you prefer.

Choosing the Motifs

Modern samplers cover a wide range of different styles and often bear little resemblance to those ladies sewed in days gone by. They are usually made from a series of motifs, and may contain wording or be surrounded by a border. The elements may share a common theme or the sampler may commemorate a special event. The possibilities for creating your own sampler are endless.

Every page of charts in this book is designed like a sampler. I tried, as far as possible, to make all the motifs on one page relate to each other, treating each page as though it were a separate design. You can make a sampler by stitching the charts as they appear on the page. For example, the Cinderella sampler on page 49 is an exact copy of the charts on page 108, and the 'Welcome to My Kitchen' sampler on page 17 is very like the chart on page 24. I hope this way of arranging the charts gives you ideas for your own sampler.

A sampler doesn't have to be an enormous project. Look at the new baby design on page 113 of the Special Days chapter. By arranging motifs vertically in the form of a band sampler, you can quickly create a small design. Use this method to make a gift instead of a card, say, for someone who loves gardening or has just moved house. The Brave Knight wall hanging on page 94 is a larger project worked in this style.

Getting Started

Once you have chosen your subject matter you will need to find a few simple materials before you can begin designing. Most important is the graph paper. I find the squares on 10 squares to the inch paper a better size than the metric versions. You can also buy sheets of tracing graph paper specially made for cross stitch that come in sizes to match the most popular fabric counts. However, these are not the best type to use for the initial stages of drafting your design.

You can draw the motifs for your project onto an A4 sheet of graph paper, but use A3 or even A2 when you come to arrange them in place. These can be purchased from most art shops or big craft stores as a pad or in sheets. An A2 sheet is useful because it can be cut down to a smaller size. Check that you use the same scale paper both to draw the motifs and for their final placement. If you intend to do lots of designing or to create a large sampler, try using a loose-leaf folder and clear plastic wallets to store your individual motifs safely together with any notes or calculations you make.

You will find the charts for the motifs used in this Victorian Parlour picture on page 20. These motifs can be used in many other ways, too.

You will need a sharp pencil (HB is best), a rubber (the designer's best friend), and a ruler for drawing borders. A fine-tipped black felt pen is useful for inking in lines once you are happy with the motifs. A compass may also be handy, but there are plenty of things around the home you can use for drawing circles and semi-circles, such as plates, tins, lids or even egg cups.

Colour pencils aren't essential unless you plan to change the colours on your motifs. If you do have the time and patience to make a full-colour version of your design, it will become something special in its own right, so sign and date it for posterity. It will also serve as a reference if you wish to repeat the design. If you have access to a computer consider buying one of the excellent design software packages available. These are not just for professional designers and are fun to use.

Try not to be too ambitious in your first attempt at designing. It's much better to have a great success with something small than to become frustrated with a big project. You may have a very clear idea of how you want your finished piece to look or it may take a lot of adjustment to get it right. When I draw my designs I always wait for the moment when everything clicks into place. Sometimes it comes quickly; at other times it takes longer. On the odd occasion when it doesn't happen at all I discard the lot. That may seem drastic, but being your own most severe critic is really the best way to produce a good design. If you are not satisfied with aspects of the composition on paper, they won't be improved by stitching them. So wait for the click.

Copy your chosen motifs carefully onto graph paper. If you are going to colour them do this before you cut them out. Sometimes you may find a motif looks better if it is reversed. To make a reversed chart, hold a small mirror next to the motif and copy the reflection. Then cut out the motifs leaving one complete square around each one. You are now ready to begin the most important stage of arranging the final design.

Design Hints

The best designs draw your eye into them. Always make sure the motifs turn in towards the centre rather than outwards and reverse any if necessary (see above). The elements of your design can be either symmetrical or asymmetrical, but you should always give thought to the balance of the finished piece. The Weather Sampler on page 81 is an example of symmetry: many of the motifs on the one side are reflected on the other. But if you study it carefully you will see a strong base line is provided by the little four season pictures and repeating suns and rainbows. The weather vane, large rainbow and thermometer give a strong central theme.

The Welcome to My Kitchen sampler on page 17 is asymmetrical. But notice how the arrangement of the horizontal and vertical motifs gives the design balance. Whichever style you choose, try not to leave large areas unstitched. Likewise, avoid the temptation to cram too many different elements into your project. With motifs of this kind it's much better to aim for a smaller design full of interest and colour.

Even if you don't plan to stitch a border, you should draw a frame and arrange your motifs carefully inside these lines. You may wish to create a border with an arched top like the Weather Sampler. To do this you need to draw a curve and square it up on your graph paper. I like to use simple straight lines and corner motifs on my designs – mainly because I don't have the patience to work out patterned borders. You will find two empty frames in the Favourite Things chapter on page 76–7. It is sometimes worth positioning one or two motifs so they appear to spill out of the main frame and add depth and interest. For example, I made the pocket watch and chain charted on page 67 trail over the edge of my Antique Collector's Cabinet opposite.

When arranging your motifs on your master sheet of graph paper make sure they are lined up with the squares. Stick into place using a non-permanent adhesive such as Spray Mount so you can reposition them if necessary. When you are happy with the design, copy it very carefully onto another sheet of graph paper to make a final stitching chart. Ink in the lines to make the chart easier to read. Compile your own key at the side if you have used a different colour scheme. If you plan to do lots of designing or to work on large projects, buy a shade card for your favourite brand of threads.

Look at the photographs throughout the book to see how you can arrange the motifs to form a sampler. Remember, being creative is all about having fun so don't worry if it takes a few attempts to get the hang of producing your own samplers and pictures – your sense of achievement will make it all worthwhile.

An Antique Collector's Cabinet was created by positioning motifs from page 67 within a frame. As an extra detail the pocket watch spills over the edge.

Materials & Techniques

When I began cross stitching you could only buy a very limited range of different fabrics.
At the time I subscribed to American stitching magazines but I could only drool over
the rainbow of different fabrics advertised in their pages. According to my mother this was
how people felt about bananas during the war. Now we have just as much choice on this side of
the Atlantic, yet we still tend to do most of our stitching on white and cream fabric. This is
probably because the same shades of thread can look so different against a coloured background
and you can't always tell how the finished stitching will look before you start.
A spirit of adventure is called for here.

Choosing a Fabric

As a designer I find a particular fabric provides the inspiration for some projects, and there is no reason why stitchers should not try the same approach. If you really like a particular colour then it is worth buying a small piece of this fabric. Sooner or later you are likely to come across a project that complements it perfectly. To test out a new fabric, sew a small block (only about 4 × 4 stitches) of each colour on a scrap of the fabric or down one edge – rather like the colour key on a painted needlepoint canvas. Study the effect to see if any shades are too close to the colour of the fabric – in which case the stitches will fade into the background. This isn't crucial on a little project, but on a large picture it could make whole areas of your careful stitching disappear into the background when the piece is viewed from a distance.

The small motifs in this book are ideal for trying out a new fabric. Designs stitched in traditional Christmas colours for example, will glow against royal blue, navy blue or black fabrics. As a general rule, if they contain lots of reds or greens, avoid using a similar shade for the background. Bright greens look even brighter against a dark green background. Deep greens look rich on a lighter or sage-green background. The same is true of reds. Pillar-box red looks stunning against grey, light blue, pale terracotta or very dark burgundy, but will be completely lost on a brighter red.

Sometimes the feel of the design will suggest what type of fabric to use. Some of the Gardening Pleasures motifs on page 18 are perfect for stitching on Rustico fabric. The subdued colours of this 'country look' also work well with many of the designs found in Home Thoughts on page 14. Designs for babies usually look better stitched on pastel colours than on white or cream. Choose big bold designs stitched on equally bright fabrics to decorate an older child's bedroom or to make a school accessory such as a shoe bag. Delicate motifs look even prettier on a soft, faded background.

To show how the choice of fabric and card mount can affect the way a design looks, I stitched the Noah's Ark from page 59 on two different fabrics. You can see opposite just how much of a difference these materials can make.

Other Surfaces for Stitching

The demand for new ways to present cross stitch has led to other non-fabric stitching materials becoming widely available. Perforated paper is one of the oldest types of craft material and would have been familiar to Victorian stitchers. Available in different colours and usually in a 14-count mesh, this durable paper can be stitched and then cut out close to the edge of the design without any risk of it fraying like fabric. Since it is stiffer than fabric, it is perfect for making Christmas decorations that need to be upright. It's also suitable for gift tags and mobiles and for covering box lids since it can be easily cut to shape with sharp scissors.

Perforated plastic is a modern variation of perforated paper that should not be confused with plastic canvas. This is available in various colours and is ideal for designs that use lots of beads. However, this material looks less attractive than perforated paper when it shows through on unstitched areas of a design.

Vinyl weave is another useful product. As its name suggests, this material looks rather like woven fabric. It is more pliable than other plastic stitching surfaces and can be wiped clean, making it ideal for kitchen or bathroom projects. Like perforated paper and plastic it can be cut to shape. It is most often used for the insert to a mug or baby 'sipper' as on page 46. Vinyl weave is also sold in sheets, usually in cream or white. It is not possible to work fractional stitches on these materials so always choose a design containing only whole cross stitch and backstitch.

If you are keen to stitch a design containing fractional stitches you will need to stiffen the fabric after you have stitched it instead of working on a non-fabric material. There are several types of Needlework Finisher and fabric stiffeners you can buy, and you should always follow the manufacturer's instructions when using these. I find a small stencil brush is the best way to apply the finisher successfully. This technique can add a whole new dimension to your stitching. All the figures for the Princess in the Tower wall hanging on page 94 were stiffened with needlework finisher.

Specially manufactured finishers can be expensive, although you only need a little. You can achieve the same effect by using ordinary, and widely available, PVA glue that dries clear. For this you will need a piece of backing fabric the same size and type as your stitched piece. Do not attempt to cut out your stitching at this stage. Cover the back of the stitching with

The choice of fabric and card mount can dramatically alter the look of a design, as these two examples show.

an even coat of PVA. If you do not have a stencil brush use a fairly stiff brush – this will help push the glue down into the stitching. Place the backing fabric onto the wrong side of the stitching taking care to smooth out any air bubbles. Add another coat of PVA to the surface of the backing and leave to dry – overnight if possible. When dry the fabric will be stiff to the touch. Now coat the front of your stitching with an even covering of PVA. Don't worry, the glue will dry clear. Once the front is dry the piece will be firm enough to cut out with sharp scissors (but don't use embroidery scissors as this may blunt them).

Basic Techniques

The designs in this book are fairly simple to stitch – even when they seem quite detailed. Many are within the reach of beginners, although some do take quite a lot of stitching. They are mainly worked in whole cross stitch, making them suitable for a wide range of fabrics.

READING THE CHARTS

The charts are printed with blocks of colour. Each coloured square on the chart represents one cross stitch. The key tells you which DMC thread numbers these colours correspond with. As a rule, each page of motifs shares the one key. However, in one or two cases, where space did not permit the inclusion of a key, it can be found on the facing page.

Knowing that some stitchers find working from colour charts difficult, I have added a symbol on top of those colours where confusion is likely to arise. Everyone sees colour differently – one person's green could be another's turquoise. If you are unsure of the exact shade of any of the unmarked colours, trust your instinct. If you think your choice will look right it probably will, and this helps develop your own eye for colour. Throughout this book I hope to encourage you to develop your own unique projects by changing colours or other details. Don't be afraid to experiment.

Some of the designs include fractional stitches. These are shown on the chart by a triangle of colour printed in one corner of the square (with the symbols when these apply). Where two different triangles share a square, make a quarter stitch in one shade and a three-quarter stitch in the other. One symbol on its own calls for a three-quarter stitch. These are not difficult to master and are explained opposite.

Backstitch brings the designs to life and should not be worked until all the other stitching is complete (see diagram opposite). I prefer to use a very dark brown for this rather than black since it is much less harsh. Where other colours are used for extra detail these will be shown in the key.

FABRIC

Most cross stitch designs are worked on evenweave fabrics. These have the same number of horizontal and vertical threads per inch. This makes them very easy to count and ensures that every stitch will come out the same size. Most people learn to cross stitch on aida, which is manufactured so that the threads are grouped in blocks. One stitch is made over each block using the holes in the fabric.

The count refers to the number of blocks (or stitches) per inch on a particular fabric. The higher the number of blocks, the smaller the design will be. For example, the same project stitched on both 14- and 16-count aida will come out larger on the lower count because it has fewer blocks per inch.

You may prefer to use one of the higher count fabrics. These are woven using single threads instead of into blocks of threads as on aida. Each cross stitch is worked over two threads on these fabrics. As a result, a project sewn over two threads on 28-count evenweave, for example, will come out the same size as if you stitched it on 14-count aida.

When buying fabric, remember it is the number of threads per inch that will determine the finished size of a project. To calculate this you will need to count how many stitches both high and wide your chosen motif is. This is the stitch count. Then divide the two measurements of the stitch count by the number of threads in your chosen fabric. When stitching a design over two threads remember to divide the stitch count by half the number of threads per inch. Always allow enough extra fabric for your chosen finishing technique.

NEEDLES AND THREADS

Use a needle for cross stitch that is blunt and slips through the fabric easily without piercing it. A size 24 or size 26 tapestry needle is best for stitching the designs in this book. Tapestry needles are graded in size, so the higher the number of a needle the finer it is. If you need to add beads to a design, a size 26 tapestry needle will pass through the eye of most beads. You can also use a smaller sharp (a fine pointed needle of the kind used for everyday sewing) if necessary.

All of the projects in this book are stitched in six-strand embroidery cotton. The size of the background fabric will determine the number of strands you should use for the best coverage. As a general rule, use three or four strands on 11-count, two strands on 14-count, 16-count and 18-count, and just one for higher counts. To achieve a smooth finish, separate the strands by pulling them one by one from the length and recombine them before threading your needle.

HOOPS AND FRAMES

You may prefer to stitch small projects without using a hoop or frame, but larger projects such as samplers or pictures do benefit from being held taut while stitching is in progress. Always remove your project from the hoop at the end of the day's stitching to prevent a ring mark from forming.

PREPARING TO STITCH

As a general rule, cut your fabric at least 7.5 cm (3 in) larger all round than the design size. Zig-zag round the edges of your fabric or bind them with masking tape (never ordinary sticky tape) to prevent them from fraying. Iron out any deep creases and find the centre by folding in four. Mark the point where the creases meet with a pin. Find the centre of your chosen design by counting how many stitches high and wide it is. Divide this in half to find the middle. Make this first stitch at the centre point of your fabric to ensure the correct placement of the design.

WORKING THE STITCHES

Cross Stitch Each cross stitch is made up of two half stitches that form a cross. At the centre of your fabric, bring the needle up in the bottom-left corner of the square you want your stitch to fill, and push it down in the top-right corner. Bring it up again in the bottom-right corner and push it down in the top left. When working a block of stitches in the same colour, stitch a line of half crosses before completing each cross on the return journey. Make sure that the top half of each cross lies in the same direction.

Quarter and Three-Quarter Stitches A three-quarter stitch is a half stitch with a quarter stitch from the centre out to one corner. It is easier to work a design containing these stitches over two threads on, say, 28-count. On aida you have to pierce the middle of the block to make a hole for your quarter stitch.

Backstitch This is an outlining stitch that can be worked diagonally, vertically or horizontally. Working back on yourself each time, bring the needle up from the underside and take it down one square back, before coming up again one square in front of the line you have completed so far.

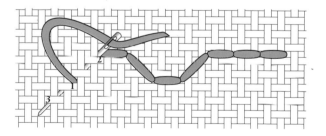

Home Thoughts

If you love stitching for your home you're sure to be tempted by the designs in this chapter. There are plenty of motifs to inspire those who enjoy cooking – in fact, everything from a wooden spoon to a splendid stove and even including the kitchen sink. Create a Victorian parlour, a pretty bathroom, a quiet study or a dream bedroom. Wherever you live, celebrate the joys of hearth and home with these special little designs.

Wooden Key Holder

This wooden key holder would make a charming housewarming gift. Using vinyl weave makes it perfect for hanging in a kitchen or a porch.

- ◆ **14-count vinyl weave**
- ◆ **Wooden Plaque to fit your chosen design**
- ◆ **Hooks**
- ◆ **Paint or varnish**
- ◆ **Decorative button (optional)**
- ◆ **PVA glue**

DESIGN NOTES

I chose a traditional inn sign shape for my key holder and painted a simple landscape to give it a country look, before varnishing it and adding the hooks. I stitched the design on page 19 on vinyl weave, cut out round it and attached it to the key holder with PVA glue. Finally, I attached a lovely hand-painted angel button to the top. Also shown is the 'Home is where your heart is' picture, created using charts from page 19. This design was cut out and stuck onto a painted and varnished wooden plaque.

Houses Wall Hanging

Combining designs within the framework of a quilt makes a wonderful wall hanging. You will find the charts for these four houses on page 18, however, the same technique could also be applied to many other motifs in the book.

- ◆ **Four stitched motifs**
- ◆ **Checked fabric for the quilt front**
- ◆ **Felt for backing**
- ◆ **Four pieces of wadding (batting) approx 13 × 13 cm (5 × 5 in)**
- ◆ **Large key charm (optional)**
- ◆ **Dowelling to hang quilt**
- ◆ **Sewing equipment**

1 Allow enough fabric for displaying on the quilt. Each design was stitched in the centre of a 15 × 15 cm (6 × 6 in) square of cream aida. Fold 6 mm (¼ in) to the back of the completed stitching. Press.

2 Plan the size of the patterned border and the spacing between the designs, using the picture for reference. Cut a piece of checked fabric the size of your quilt, adding a 6 mm (¼ in) seam allowance.

3 Tack a piece of wadding to the wrong side of each of the stitched squares and pin them in position on top of the checked fabric. Slipstitch them neatly in place and remove the tacking.

4 Turn under the seam allowance on each side of the front and press. Then turn under a further 2.5 cm (1 in) along the top and press. Sew two lines of stitching across the fabric to make a channel for the dowelling.

5 Cut a piece of felt for the backing and slipstitch the two pieces of the hanging together.

OPPOSITE: Welcome to my Kitchen Sampler. This sampler was created from the motifs charted on page 24 with some additions, and stitched on 14-count cream aida. Another ideal gift for a new home is the welcome card, using motifs from page 19, cut out and stuck to the front of plain card.

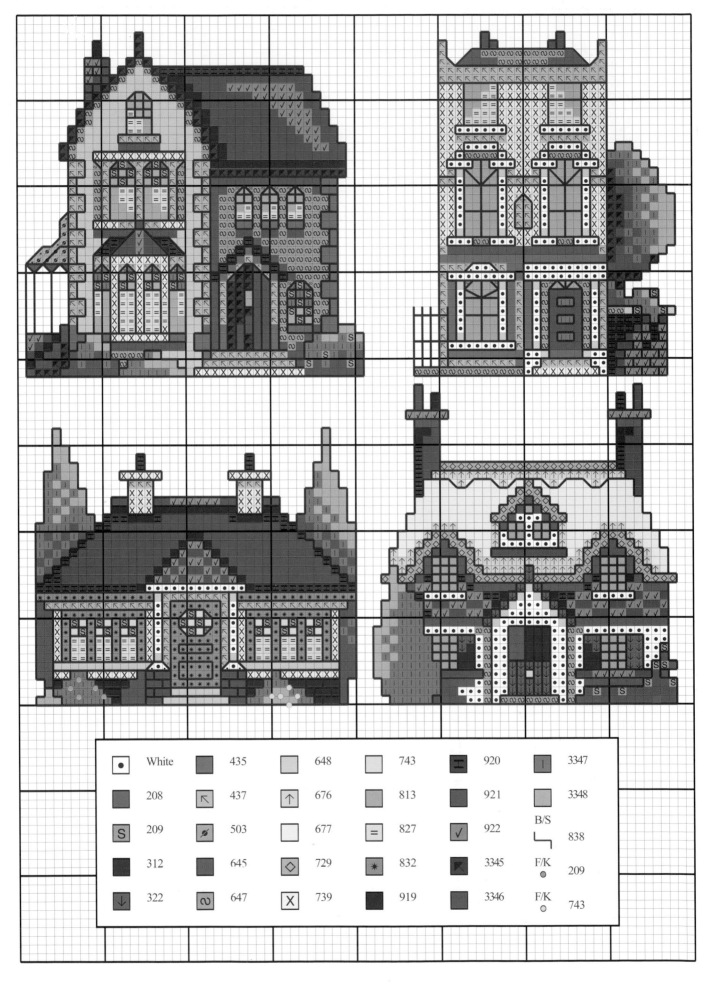

•	White		435		648		743	⊥	920	∣	3347
	208	↖	437	↑	676		813		921		3348
S	209	⊘	503		677	=	827	√	922	B/S	838
	312		645	◇	729	∗	832	◤	3345	F/K ●	209
↓	322	∽	647	X	739		919		3346	F/K ●	743

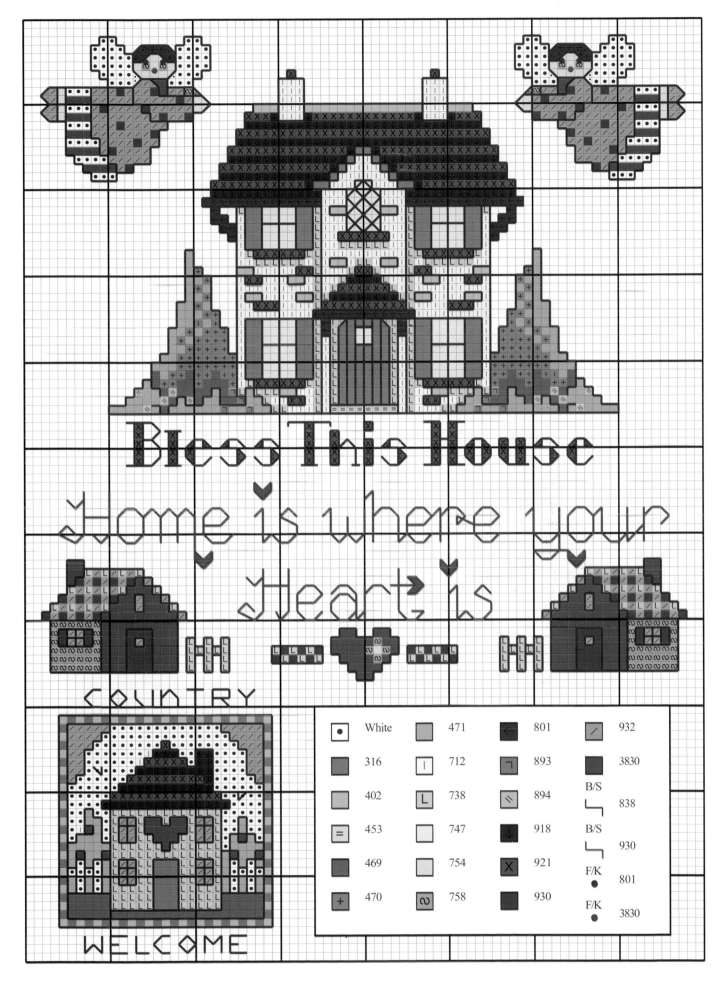

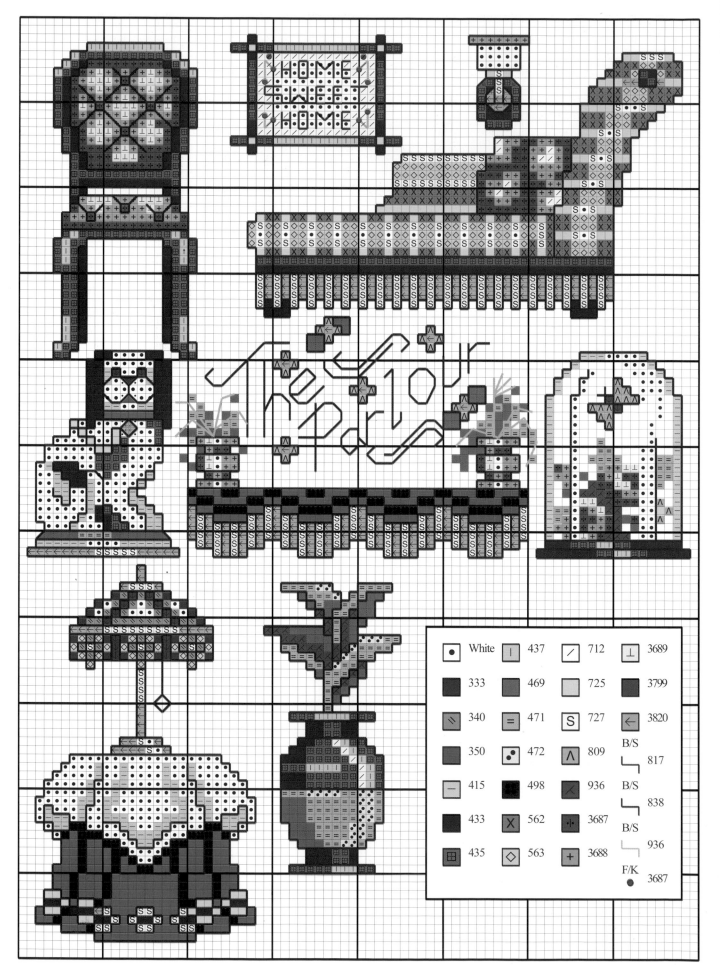

●	White	I	437	/	712	⊥	3689
■	333	■	469		725	■	3799
⧅	340	=	471	S	727	←	3820
■	350	⊙	472	∧	809		B/S
							817
—	415	■	498	↖	936		B/S
							838
■	433	X	562	⊡	3687		B/S
⊞	435	◇	563	+	3688		936
							F/K
						●	3687

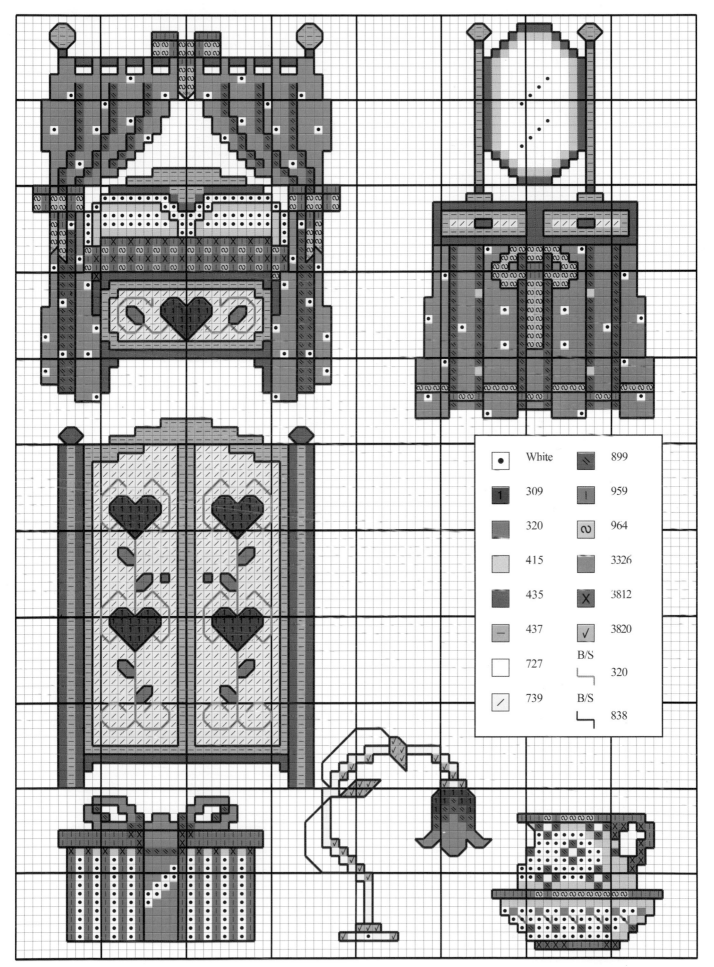

•	White	⁄⁄	899
1	309	I	959
	320	2	964
	415		3326
	435	X	3812
—	437	√	3820
	727	B/S	320
⁄	739	B/S	838

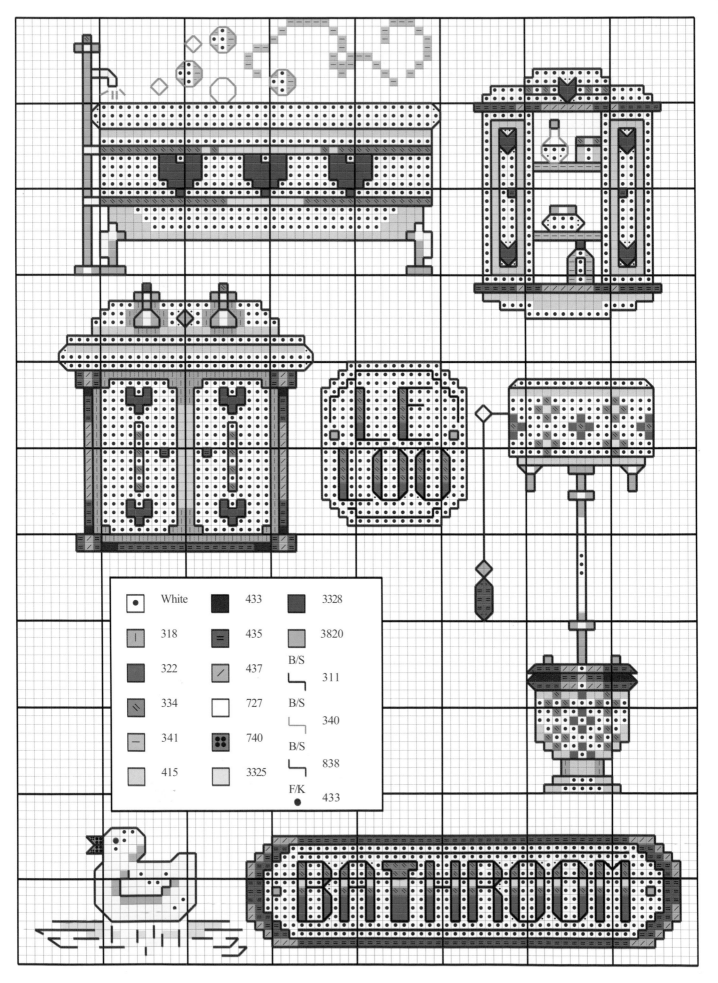

	White		433		3328
	318		435		3820
	322		437	B/S	311
	334		727	B/S	340
	341		740	B/S	838
	415		3325	F/K	433

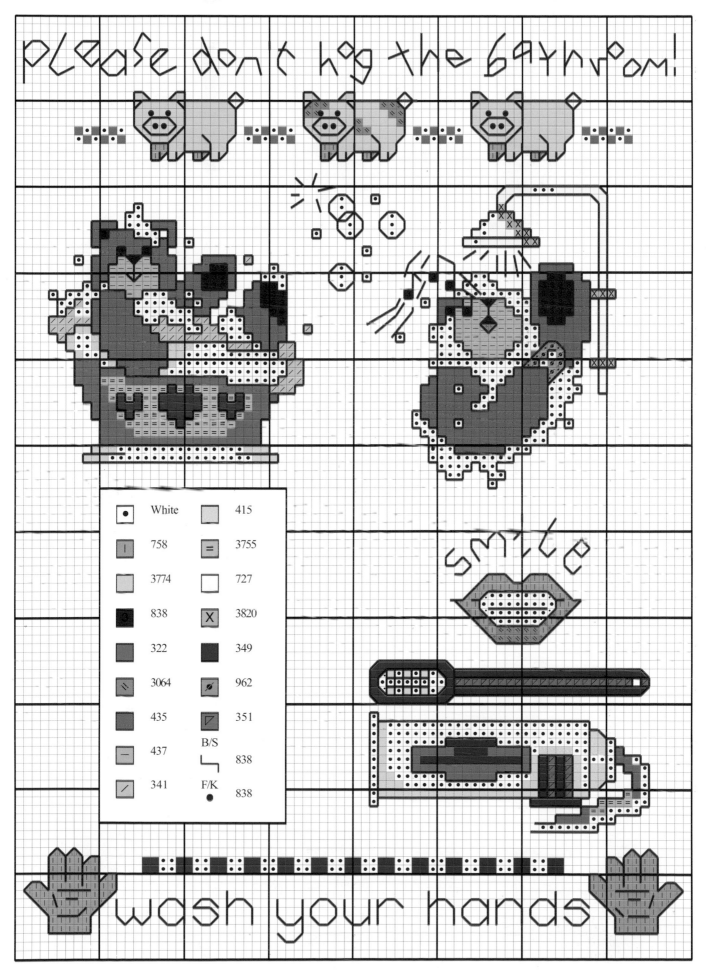

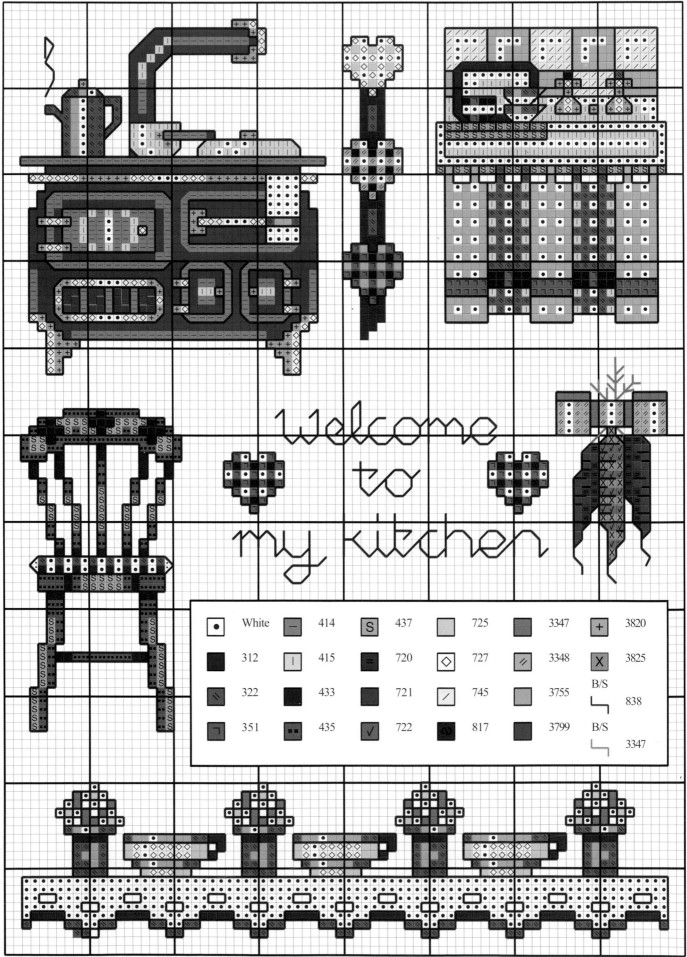

	White		414	S	437		725		3347	+	3820
	312	I	415	=	720	◇	727	//	3348	X	3825
	322		433		721	/	745		3755	B/S ⌐	838
⌐	351		435	√	722		817		3799	B/S ⌐	3347

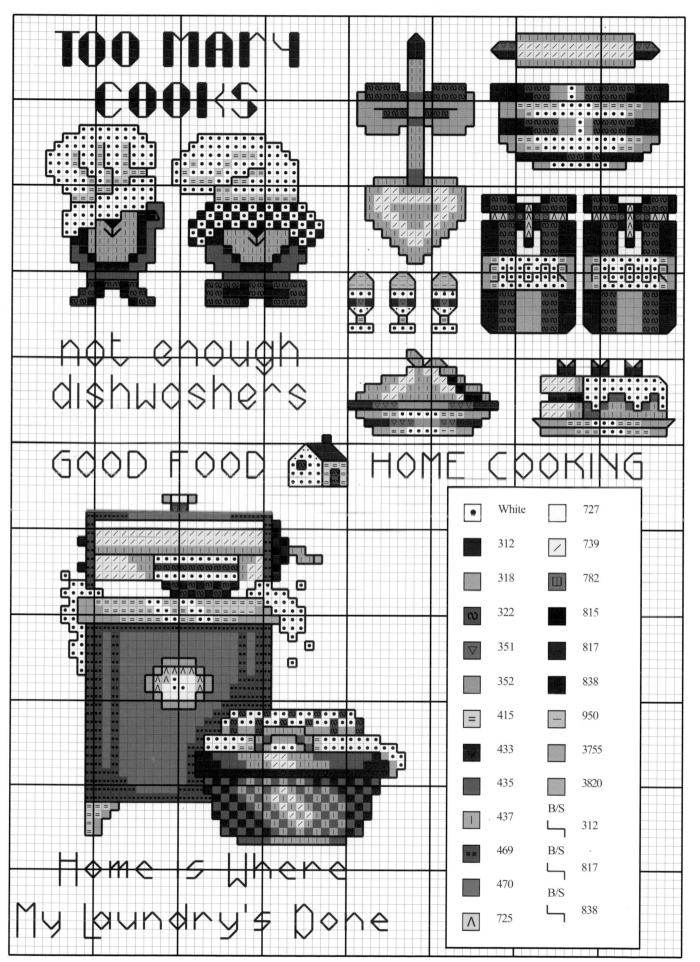

TOO MANY COOKS

not enough dishwashers

GOOD FOOD   HOME COOKING

Home is Where

My Laundry's Done

White		727	
312		739	
318		782	
322		815	
351		817	
352		838	
415		950	
433		3755	
435		3820	
437		B/S 312	
469		B/S 817	
470		B/S 838	
725			

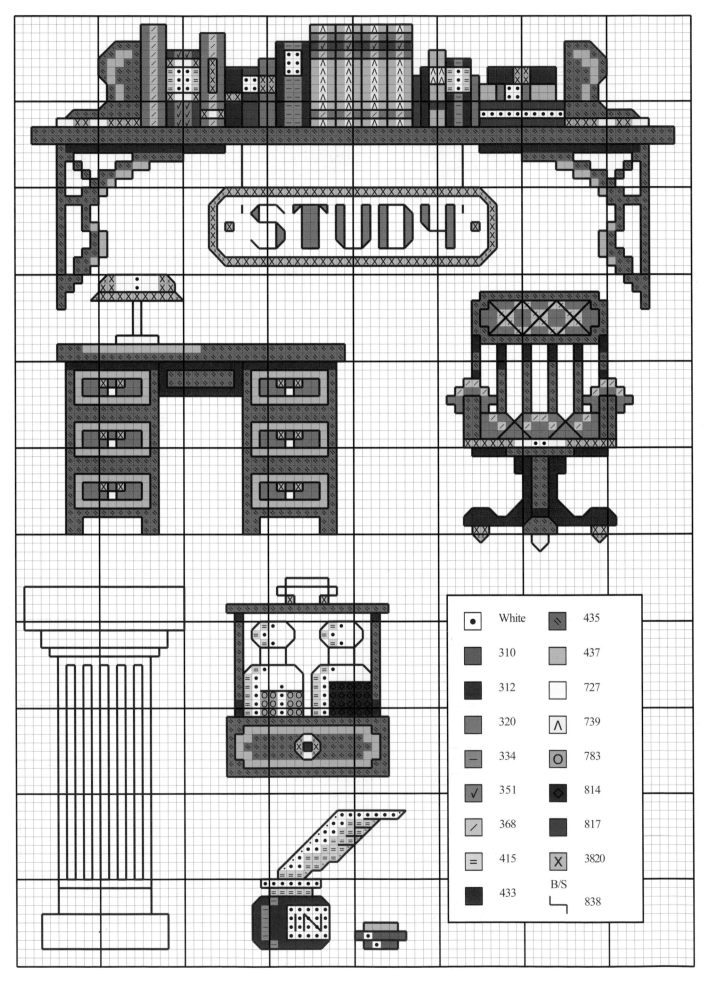

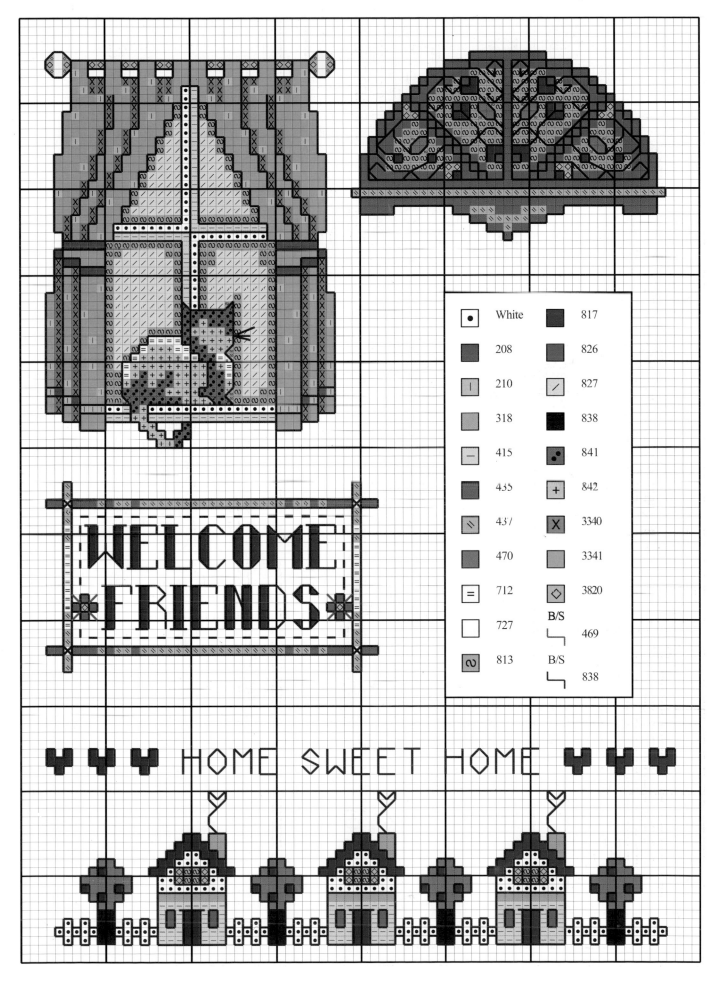

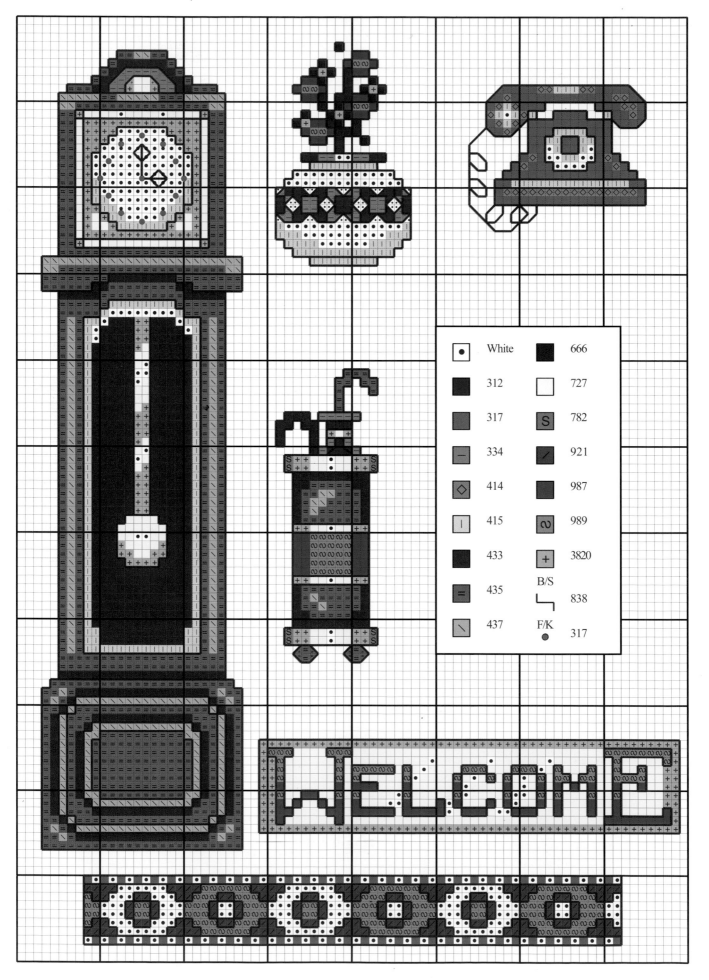

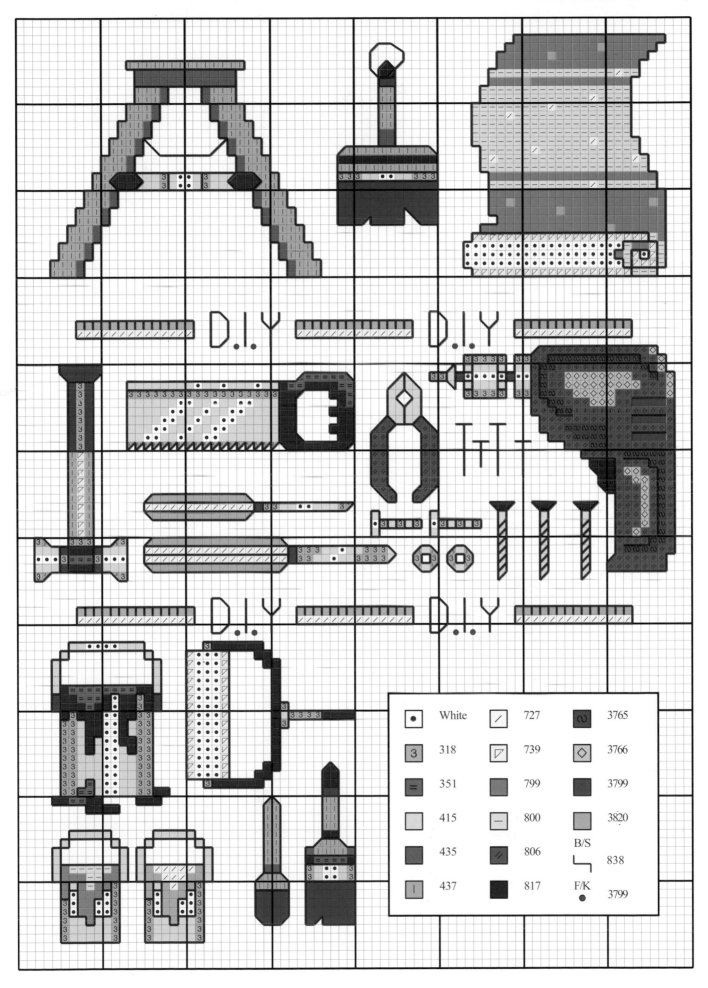

	White		727		3765
3	318		739		3766
=	351		799		3799
	415	—	800		3820
	435		806	**B/S**	
	437		817	⌐	838
				F/K ●	3799

For a lawn
without
weeds
sew
stitches
not seeds

Gardening Pleasures

In this chapter you will find dozens of ways to delight a keen gardener. There's everything from flowers to fresh veggies, all ready and waiting to be recreated in stitches. Choose from the beautiful topiaries, rose-covered bower and sundial of a formal garden, or capture the feel of a country garden with its picket fence, quaint birdhouse and beehives. There's even a pair of wellies waiting to be put on.

Gardener's Quilted Wall Hanging

*Here's a wonderful design to make for a keen gardener—a beautiful quilted wall hanging
stitched with images of the many pleasures their garden brings.*

- ◆ **Cream 14-count aida**
- ◆ **Print fabric for the quilt front**
- ◆ **Felt for backing**
- ◆ **Wadding (batting)**
- ◆ **Buttons, charms, and ribbon (optional)**
- ◆ **Sewing equipment**
- ◆ **Dowelling**

DESIGN NOTES

The seven motifs that appear on this hanging were
taken from the charts on pages 34–43. You can
either stitch each design on a separate piece of fabric as I did, allowing 5 cm (2 in) all round each one,
or work them all together on a single piece of aida.
Turn to pages 6–9 for advice on how to chart a master design. When using this method remember to
leave a 5 cm (2 in) gap between each one.

MAKING UP THE HANGING

1 To fringe the edges of each stitched piece,
make a straight line of stay stitching about 2.5
cm (1 in) away from the design. This will lock the
weave of the fabric in place, allowing you to fray the
fabric threads up to that line and no further. It is
much easier to do this is on a sewing machine, but
a line of closely-spaced backstitching will also work.
Fray the aida up to that line, then trim the fringed
edges to the right length.

2 Lay out your stitched pieces on the hanging
and decide where they should go. Decide how
big the print fabric border should be, referring to
the photograph if you need to. You can now work
out the size to cut your fabric for the quilt front.
Add an extra 6 mm (¼ in) all round for joining it to

the felt backing. Zig zag around the edge of this
piece of fabric (or for the minimum of sewing, cut
with pinking shears) as it will be folded to the back.
Arrange and pin (or tack) your stitched pieces to the
right side of the fabric.

3 Cut a piece of wadding (batting) slightly smaller than this piece of fabric. Pin the wadding
(batting) to the wrong side of the fabric then tack
(baste) securely in place. Now quilt around your
motifs, by taking small stab stitches just inside the
fringed edge, passing through all the layers. When
all of the motifs are quilted onto the fabric in this
way remove the tacking. Next attach any buttons,
charms or other decorations. Cut a piece of felt for
the backing 6 mm (¼ in) smaller all round than
your quilted piece. Pin this in place on the wrong
side of the quilted piece. Turn the seam allowance
neatly onto the felt backing (press in place if
desired) then slipstitch the pieces together.

4 The hanging tabs are cut from felt to keep
down the amount of sewing. Decide what size
the tabs will be and if you want to shape the ends.
Measure the distance between them carefully and
and mark with pins. Stitch one end securely to the
backing felt then bring the other end to the front.
Stitch this end in place and finish off by adding a
decorative button or ribbon on top.

Picket Fence

Here's an unusual way to bring the garden indoors. Stitch a series of gardening motifs and use them to embellish a little wooden picket fence.

- ◆ **Cream 14-count aida**
- ◆ **Needlework Finisher or other fabric stiffener**
- ◆ **Wooden fence**
- ◆ **Paint or varnish for the fence**
- ◆ **Clear glue**

DESIGN NOTES

The little piece of wooden fencing forms the basis of this project. This came from Hantex Ltd (see stockists on page 127) who have a wonderful selection of interesting pieces to inspire unusual projects. The fence is supplied unpainted so you can either paint it in the colour of your choice or just give it a coat of clear varnish. You could also try making your own fence from a piece of card. The motifs were all taken from this chapter and were treated with a coat of Needlework Finisher (see page 11 for more information about this technique) and cut to shape. They were attached to the fence using clear glue.

Plant Poke

This charming little plant poke will look good nestling among the pot plants in your living room.

- ◆ **Perforated paper**
- ◆ **Wooden plant poke**
- ◆ **Paint or varnish**
- ◆ **Ribbon and/or button**
- ◆ **Craft knife or sharp scissors**
- ◆ **Clear glue**

1 First lay the plant poke onto the perforated paper and carefully draw round the shape with a pencil, making sure you do not press too hard and damage the surface. Use this line to position your stitching correctly. Paint or varnish your plant poke and allow to dry.

2 When the stitching is complete, cut out the shape just outside the pencil line using a craft knife or sharp scissors. Carefully erase the pencil line using a very soft rubber.

3 Run a line of clear glue around the edge of the plant poke and a much thinner layer across the centre and allow it to become slightly tacky before positioning the stitching on top. Trim any excess paper from the edge. Finish by tying or sticking a ribbon bow to the stem of the plant poke.

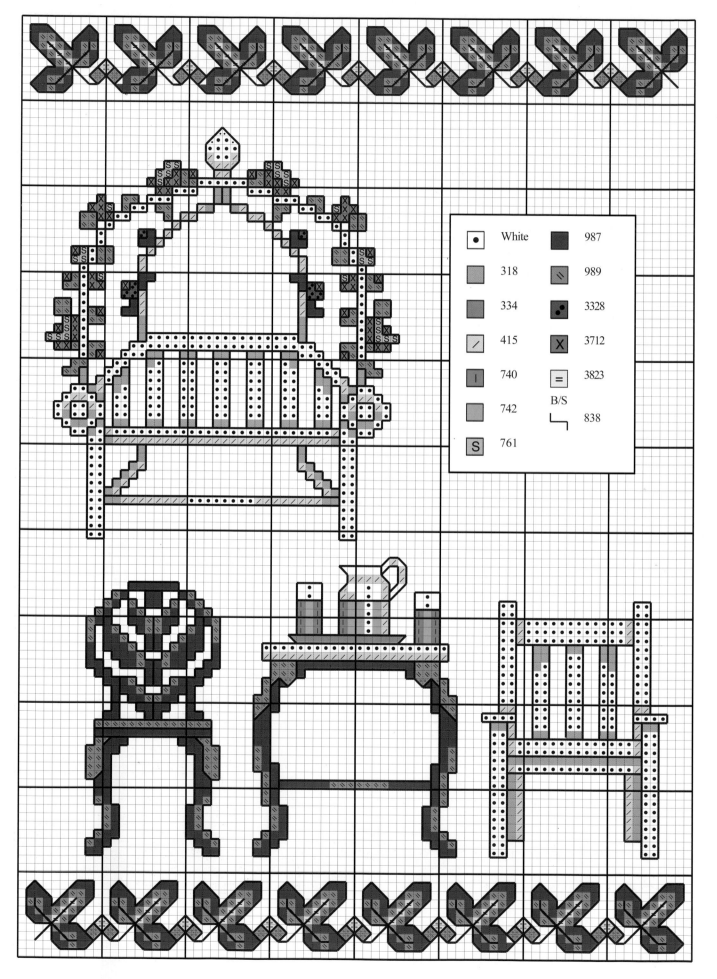

	White		987
	318		989
	334		3328
/	415	X	3712
I	740	=	3823
	742	B/S	
S	761		838

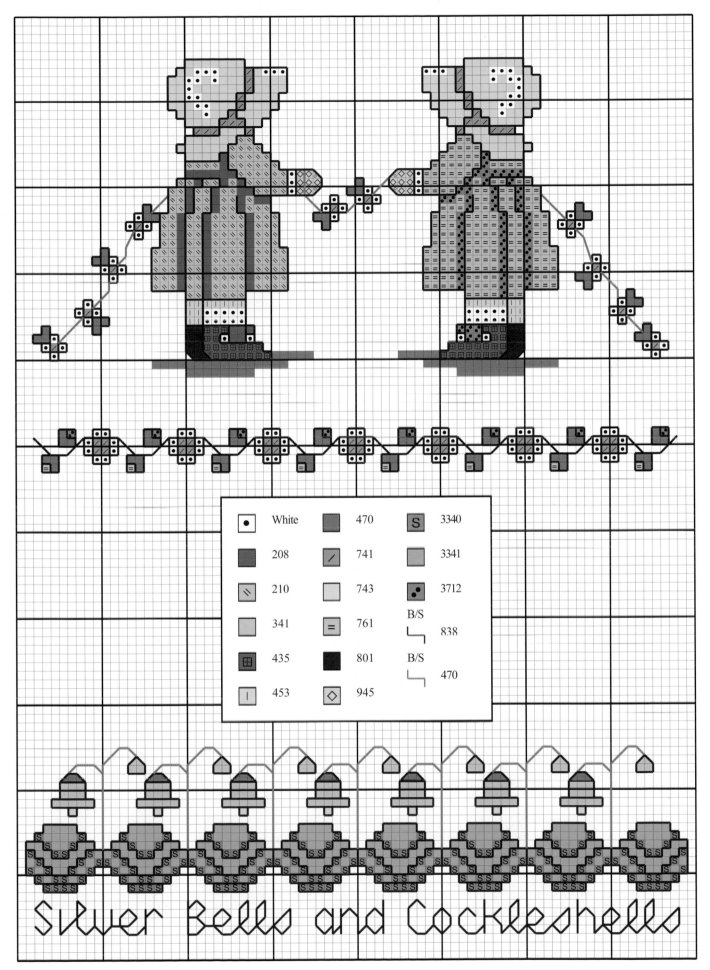

•	White		470	S	3340	
	208	/	741		3341	
	210		743	•	3712	
	341	=	761	B/S ⌐	838	
	435		801	B/S ⌐	470	
I	453	◇	945			

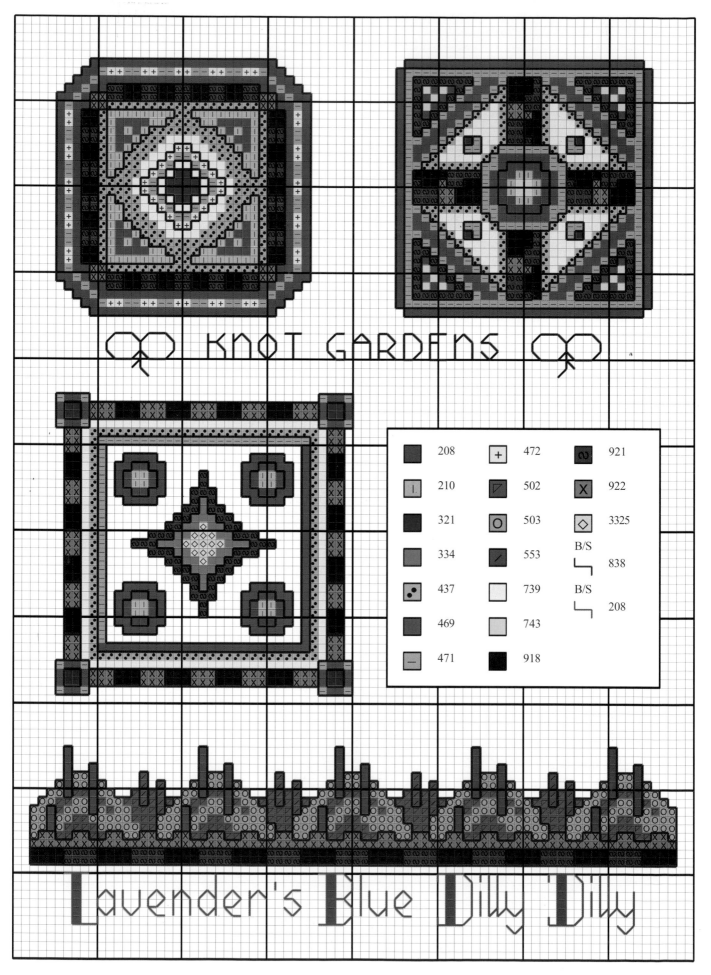

KNOT GARDENS

■	208	⊞	472	∞	921
▣	210	◨	502	☒	922
■	321	Ⓞ	503	◇	3325
■	334	◿	553	B/S ⌐	838
∴	437	▢	739	B/S ⌐	208
■	469	▨	743		
▭	471	■	918		

Lavender's Blue Dilly Dilly

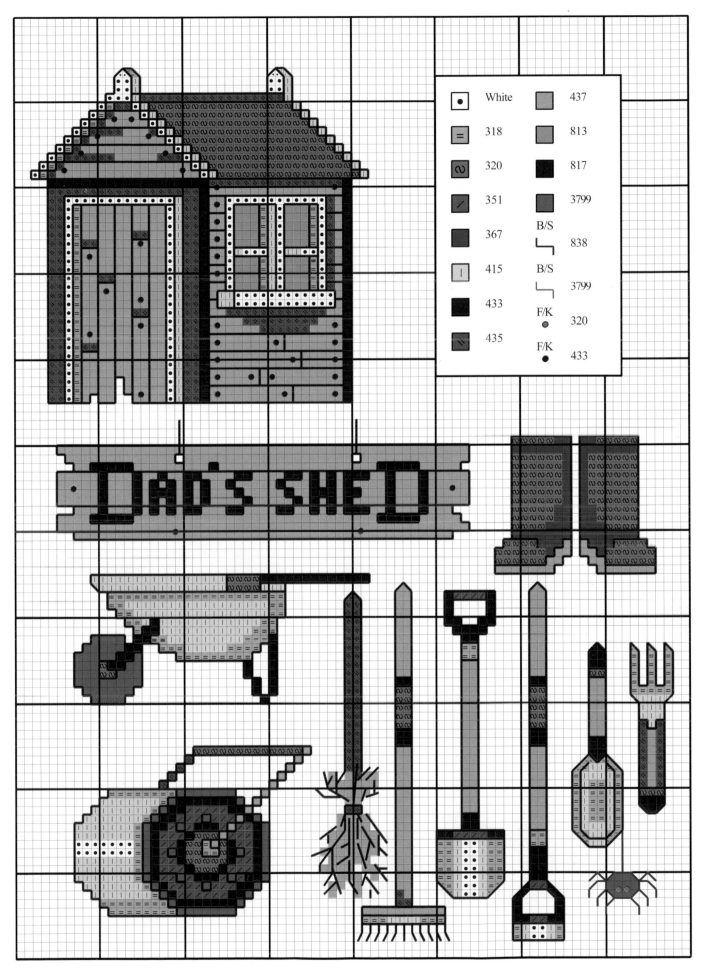

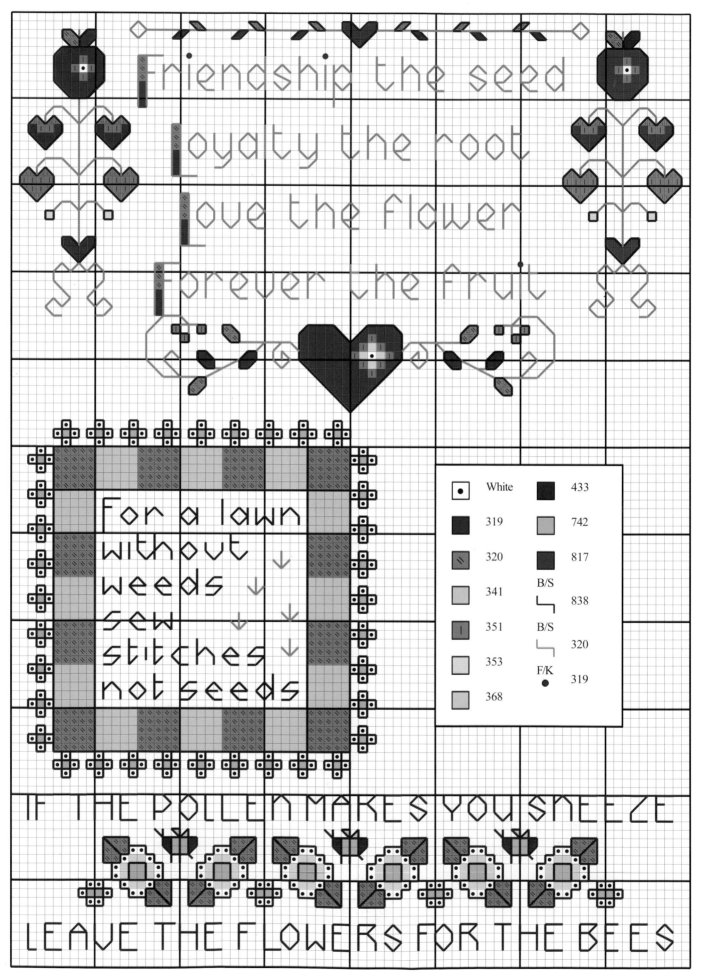

Friendship the seed

Loyalty the root

Love the flower

Forever the fruit

For a lawn
without
weeds
sew
stitches
not seeds

	White		433
	319		742
	320		817
	341	B/S	
	351		838
	353	B/S	
	368		320
		F/K	319

IF THE POLLEN MAKES YOU SNEEZE

LEAVE THE FLOWERS FOR THE BEES

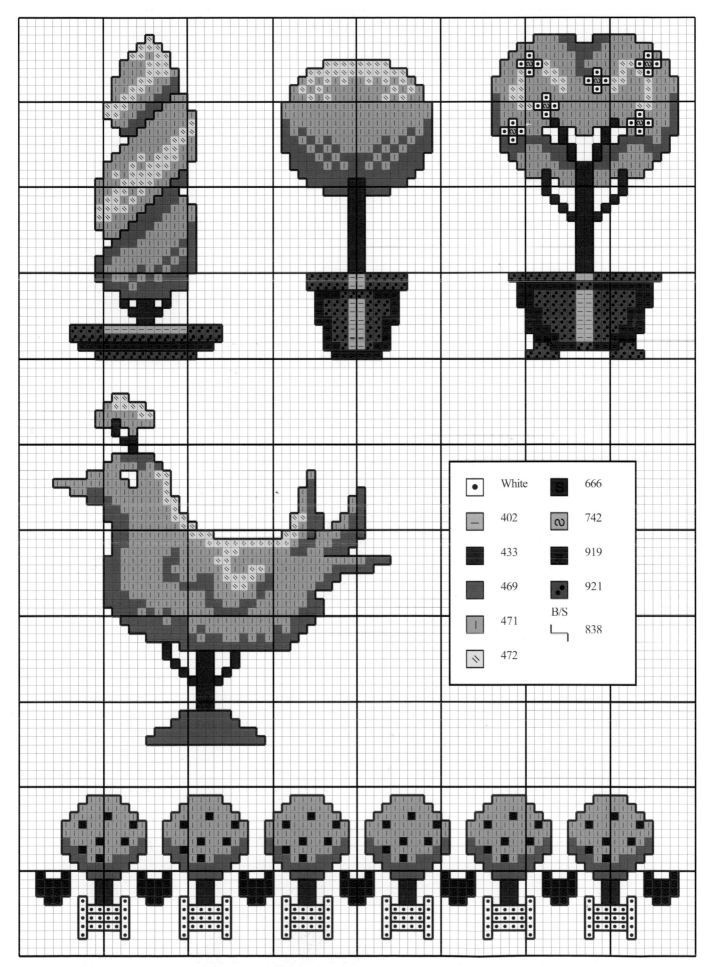

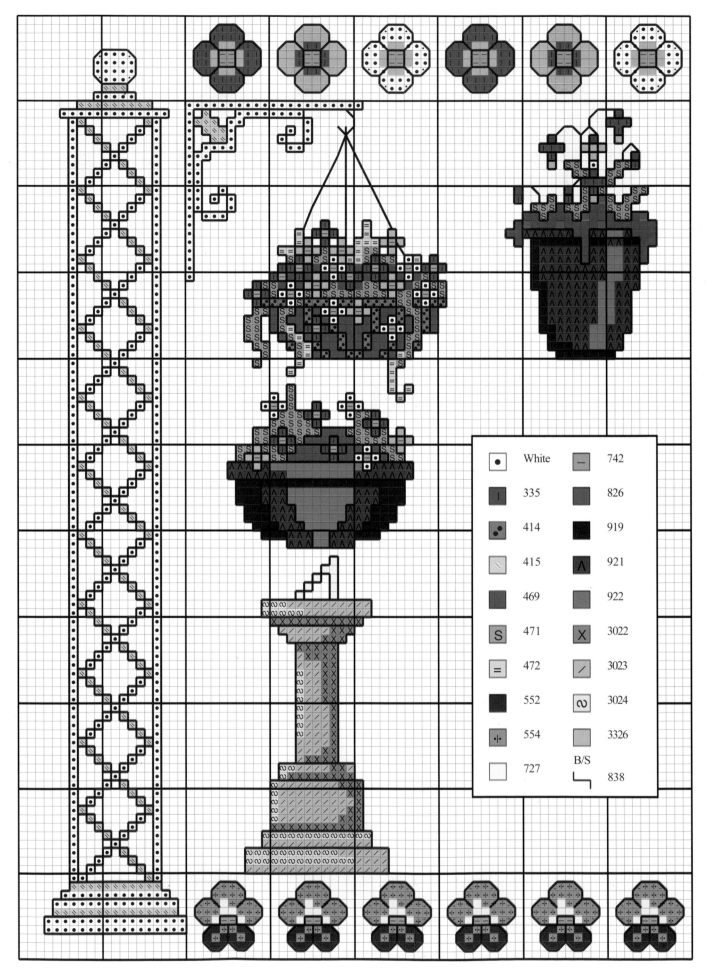

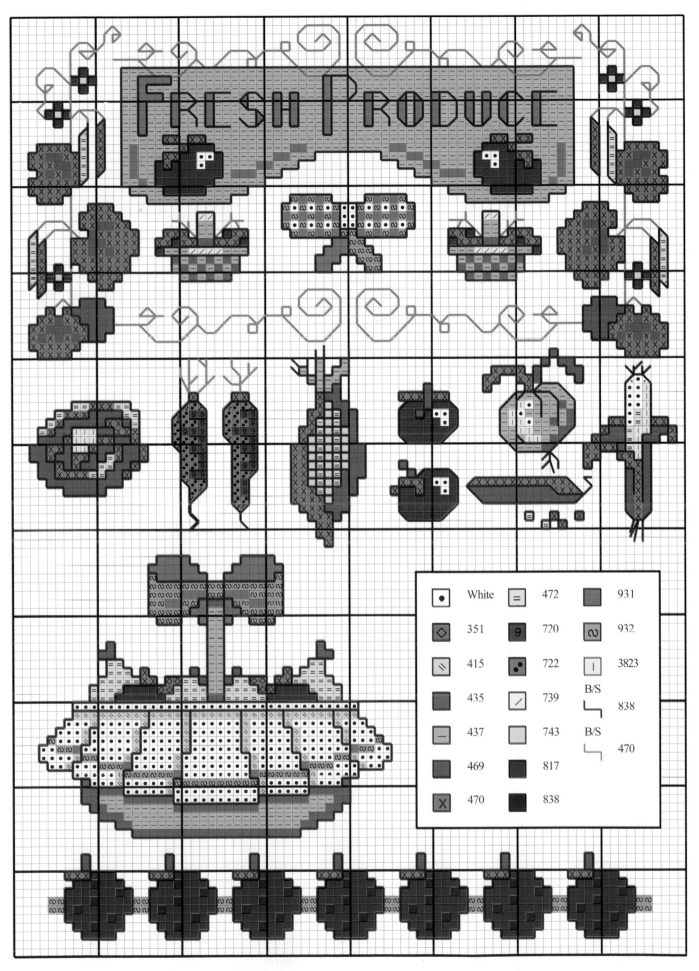

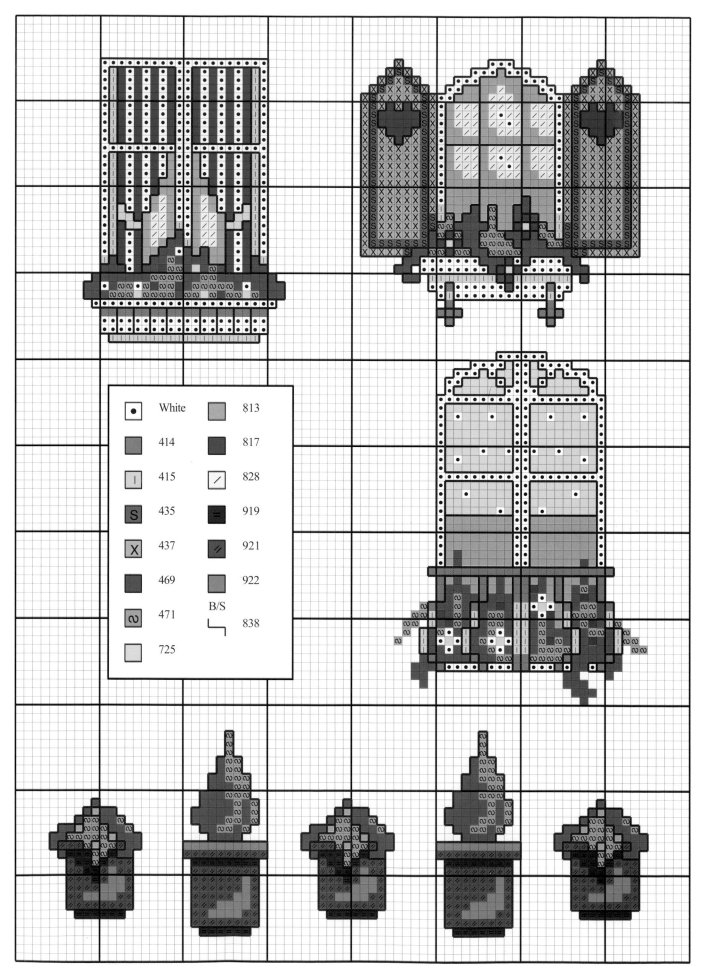

White

414

415

S 435

X 437

469

471

725

813

817

828

919

921

922

B/S

838

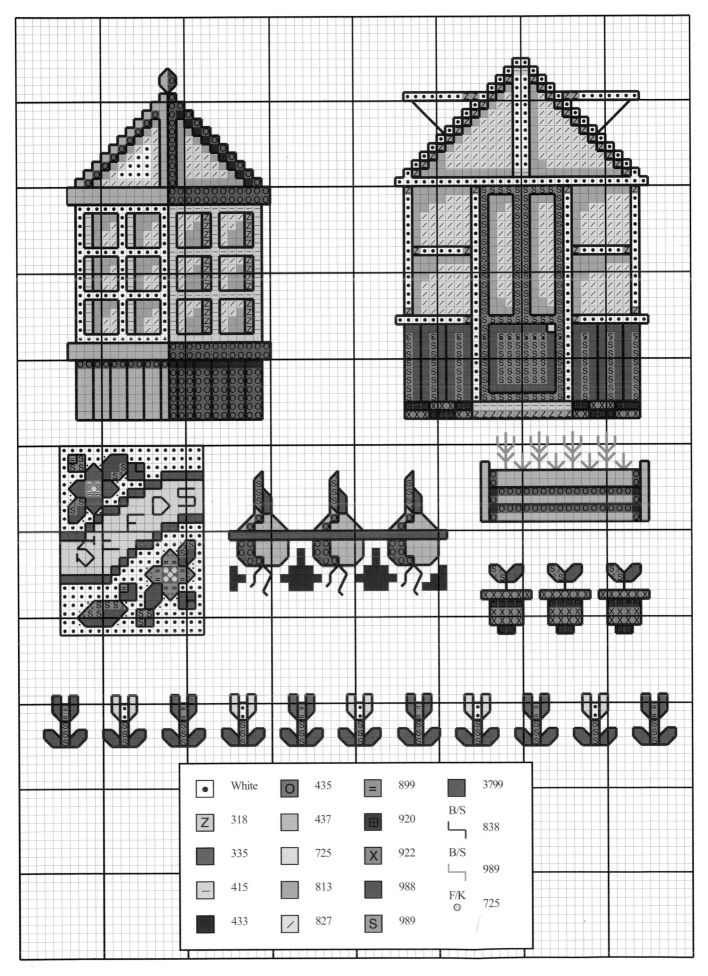

•	White	O	435	=	899	▨	3799
Z	318	▨	437	⊞	920		B/S
▨	335	▢	725	X	922	⌐	838
—	415	▨	813	▨	988		B/S
▨	433	╱	827	S	989	⌐	989
						F/K	
						○	725

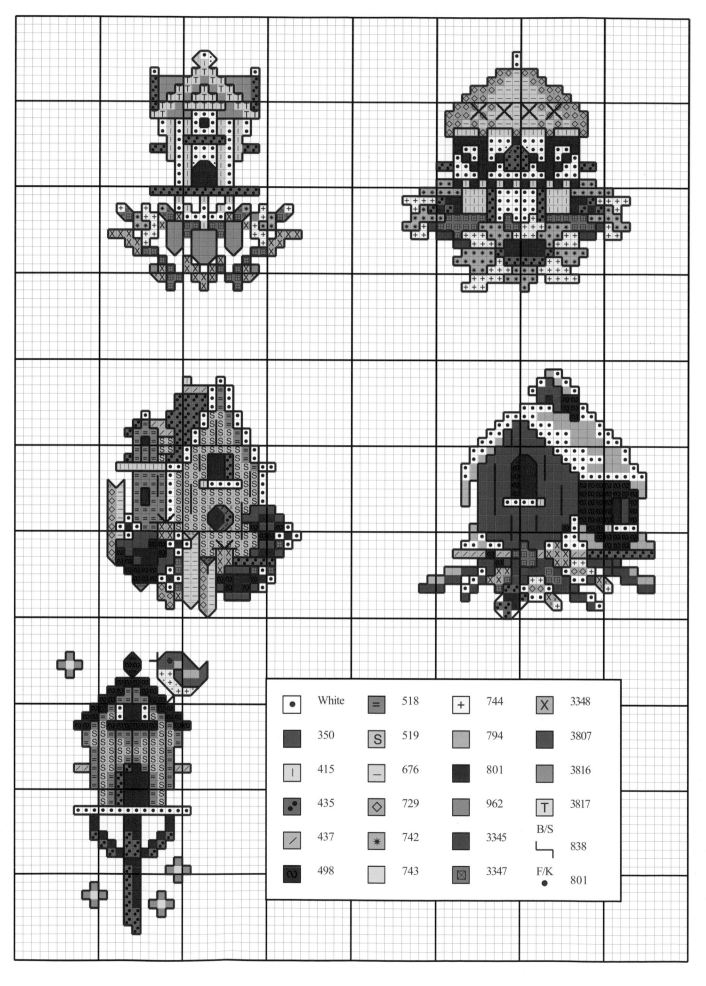

•	White	=	518	+	744	X	3348
	350	S	519		794		3807
l	415	—	676		801		3816
•	435	◇	729		962	T	3817
/	437	✳	742		3345		B/S
							838
∽	498		743	⊠	3347		F/K
						•	801

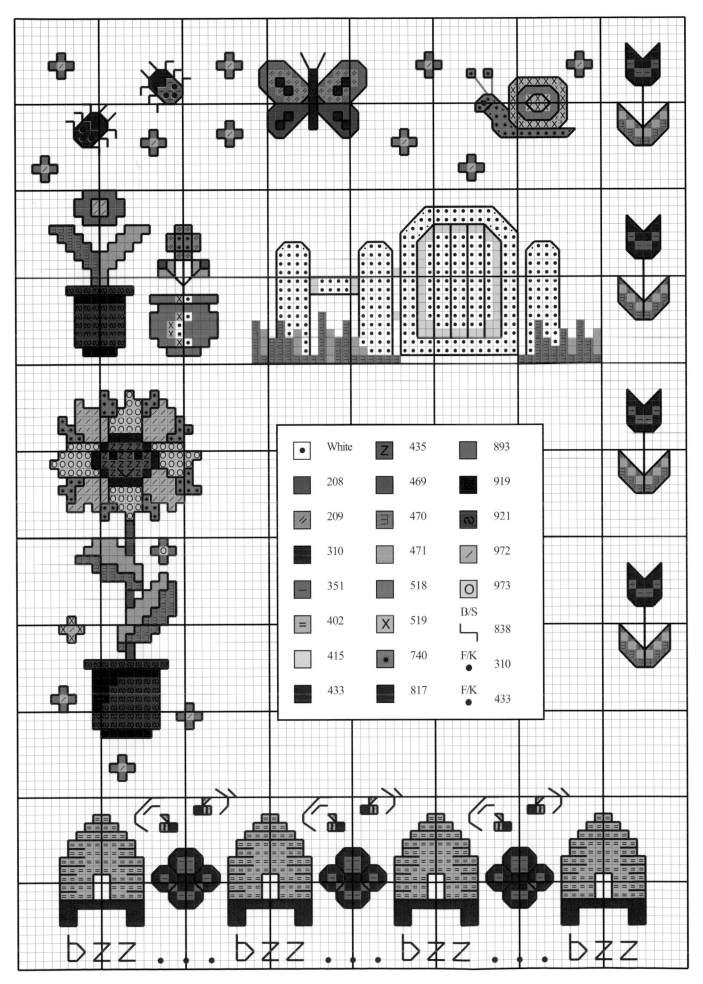

Childhood Days

These designs capture the precious days of childhood and are perfect for embellishing gifts for the little ones in your life. Decorate a nursery item or some tiny clothes with trains, Noah's Ark figures or favourite toys. Stitch a charming picture of a boy or girl for proud grandparents or to say 'thank you' to teacher. Let these designs carry you back to carefree days as you create items children will treasure even after they are grown.

Nursery Cushions

These delightful cushions would make an ideal christening gift for a baby. They are stitched on Afghan cloth and feature some of the nursery motifs in this chapter.

- ◆ **Afghan fabric**
- ◆ **Fabric for backing**
- ◆ **Decorative buttons (optional)**
- ◆ **Good quality filling**
- ◆ **Sewing equipment**

DESIGN NOTES

You can buy squares of Afghan fabric suitable for making cushions. I used 18-count Anne cloth. This is perfect for a cushion front and gives you four squares to fill with motifs. Stitch the designs over two threads using three strands for cross stitch and one strand for backstitch. Check your chosen motifs will fit the squares and centre each one within a square. If you intend to fill all four squares, check the design will be balanced before you start and reverse any of the motifs if necessary (see page 8). I used the Noah's Ark figures from page 59 on one cushion and the Baby's Room motifs from page 51 on the other. To finish off, I added some decorative buttons but you may wish to omit these if the cushion will be handled by very small children.

MAKING THE CUSHION

When you have completed the stitching cut a piece of backing fabric the same size and join the two with right sides facing, leaving an opening for turning. Trim the seams, turn, press if necessary and stuff firmly with good quality filling (the kind used for toys is best). Slipstitch the opening together.

Giraffe Pram Toy

Here's a lovely way to present one of the nursery motifs in this chapter. The giraffe has been made up into a soft toy baby is sure to enjoy cuddling.

- ◆ **White 22-count Hardanger fabric**
- ◆ **Good quality cotton fabric for backing**
- ◆ **Toy filling**
- ◆ **Sewing equipment**
- ◆ **Soft pencil (B or 2B)**

1 Centre and stitch the Giraffe design from page 51 on the Hardanger allowing an extra 7.5 cm (3 in) all round.

2 Cut a piece of backing fabric the same size as the stitching. Choose a washable fabric especially if the toy will be handled by a baby.

3 Place the stitched piece and backing fabric right sides together and pin firmly.

4 Using a soft pencil, lightly draw around the outline of the giraffe following his shape and leaving a space of about 5–6cm (2–2.5in) round the design. This will be your stitching line. Machine stitch around this line leaving a large enough gap for turning.

5 Trim away the excess fabric, turn, stuff firmly with toy filling and slipstitch the opening together.

Baby Accessories

These nursery items are sure to be treasured long after baby has grown up. They have all been personalised with motifs from this chapter and are sure to raise a smile at mealtimes.

◆ **Baby's bib with ready-to-sew aida insert**
   ◆ **Sipper cup with vinyl weave insert**

These two designs, stitched using motifs from the Land of Dreams chapter on page 94, are suitable for older children. The Cinderella Sampler was stitched straight from the chart on page 108. It was sewn over two threads on 28-count cream evenweave with a gold lurex thread woven through it. For the Shoe House Cushion, the design on page 103 was stitched in the centre of a 26cm (10in) square of lemon 14-count aida. The design was trimmed with decorative buttons and made into a simple cushion.

DESIGN NOTES

The opening pages of this chapter show just two of the items you can buy ready to stitch a motif on as a gift for a baby or child, and many other items are available. Some of the smaller items, such as bootees, can be fiddly to sew, but they make lovely gifts and are well worth the effort. These projects feature the Toy Train from page 58 and the Hungry Baby from page 60. Check that your chosen motif fits nicely within the space provided before you start stitching. Why not stitch a set of these items using matching motifs, and place them in a pretty basket as a special present for a new mum.

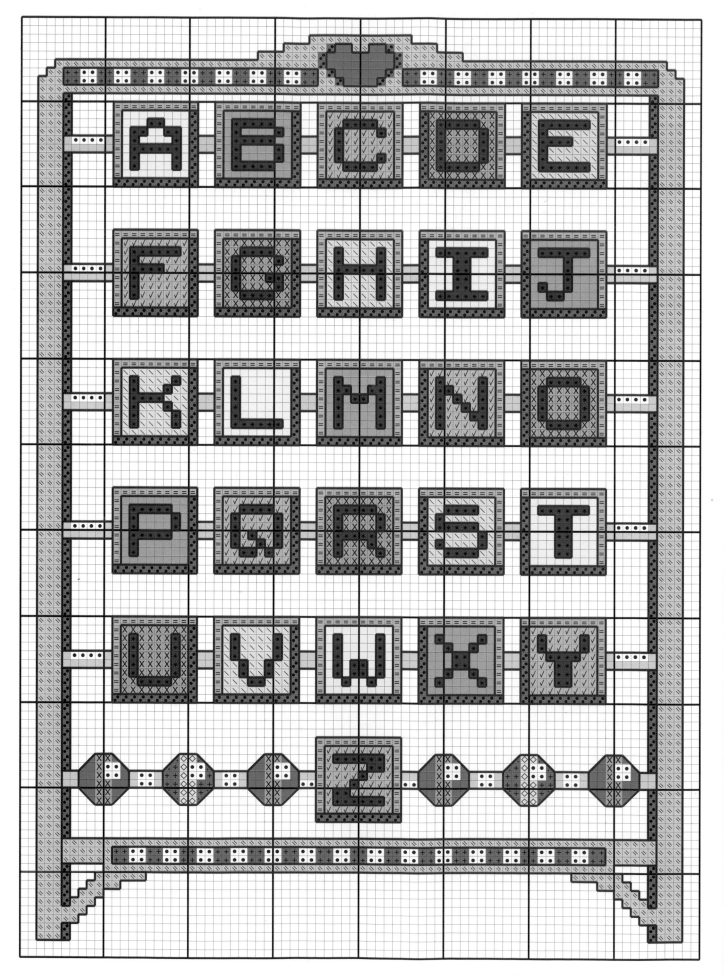

•	White	\\	564		826
	209	∽	597		838
—	211	/	603	◇	3325
✳	312	\\	738		3328
+	334	⊥	740		3811
	415	←	742		3823
	433		744	B/S	
••	435	✕	760	⌐	838
=	437	✓	813	F/K •	838

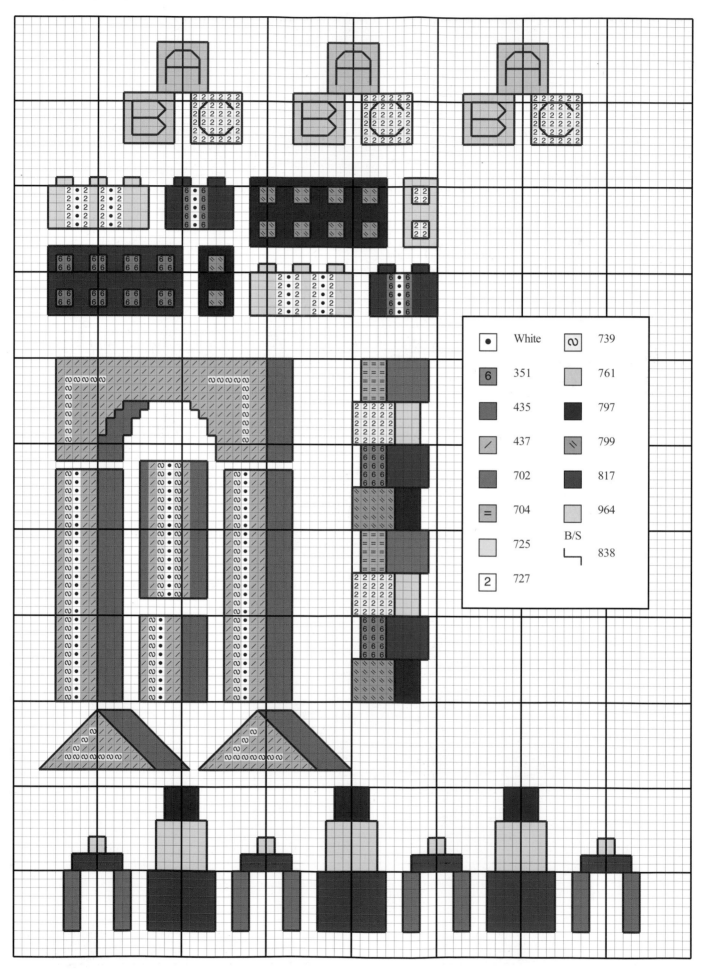

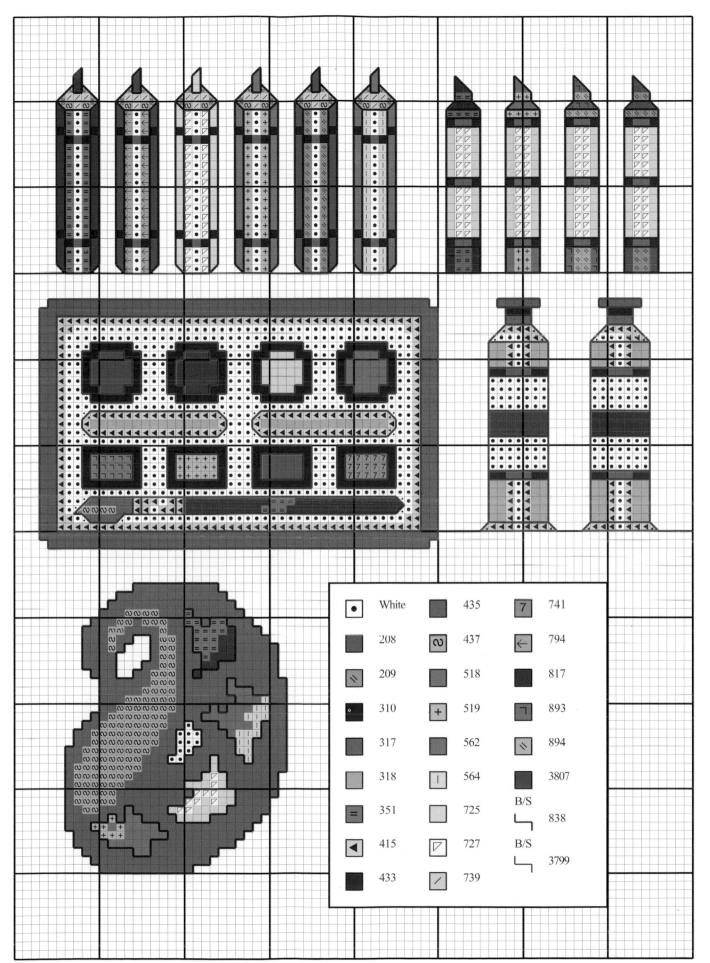

•	White		435	7	741
	208	⌀	437	←	794
╲	209		518		817
•	310	+	519	⌐	893
	317		562	╲	894
	318	|	564		3807
=	351		725	B/S └	838
◀	415	◱	727	B/S └	3799
	433	╱	739		

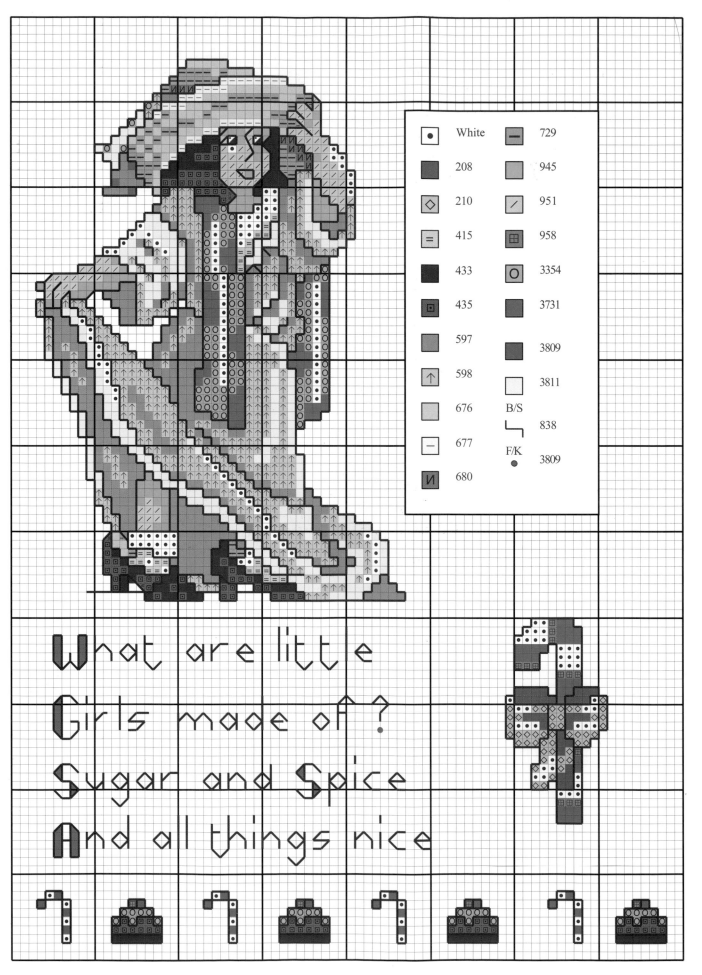

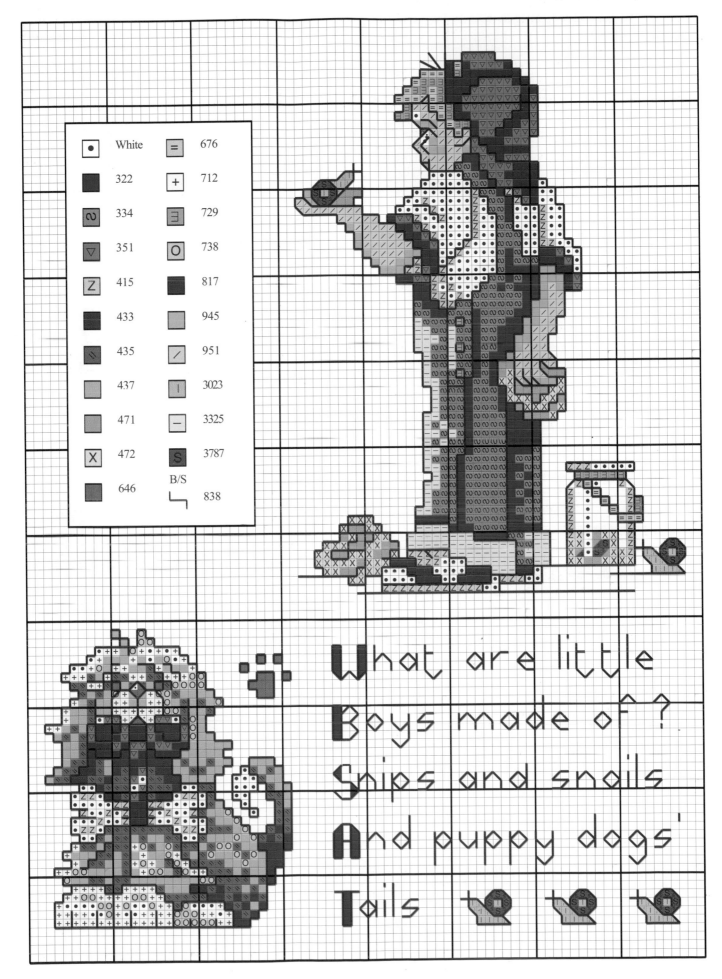

What are little
Boys made of?
Snips and snails
And puppy dogs'
Tails

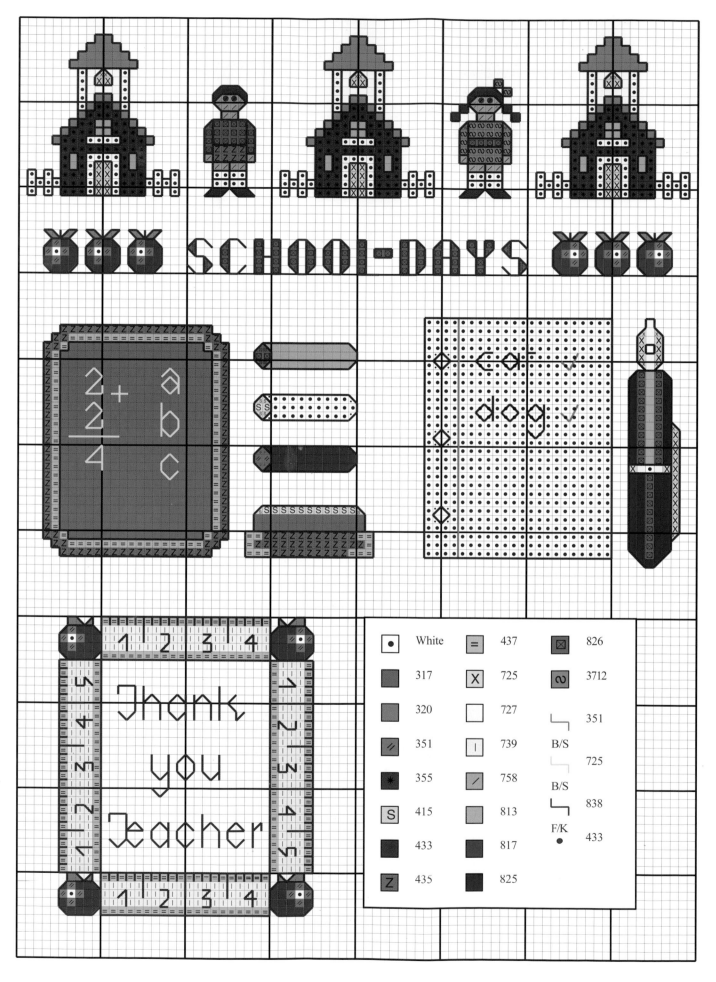

•	White	=	437	⊠	826
	317	X	725	∽	3712
	320		727	⌐	351
╱╱	351	|	739	B/S	
✳	355	╱	758		725
S	415		813	B/S	
	433		817	⌐	838
Z	435		825	F/K	
				•	433

	White		Z	761
=	415			792
	433		∞	793
I	435			794
	437		X	838
	740		/	945
X	742			951
*	744			3328
	746		B/S	839
	760		F/K	838

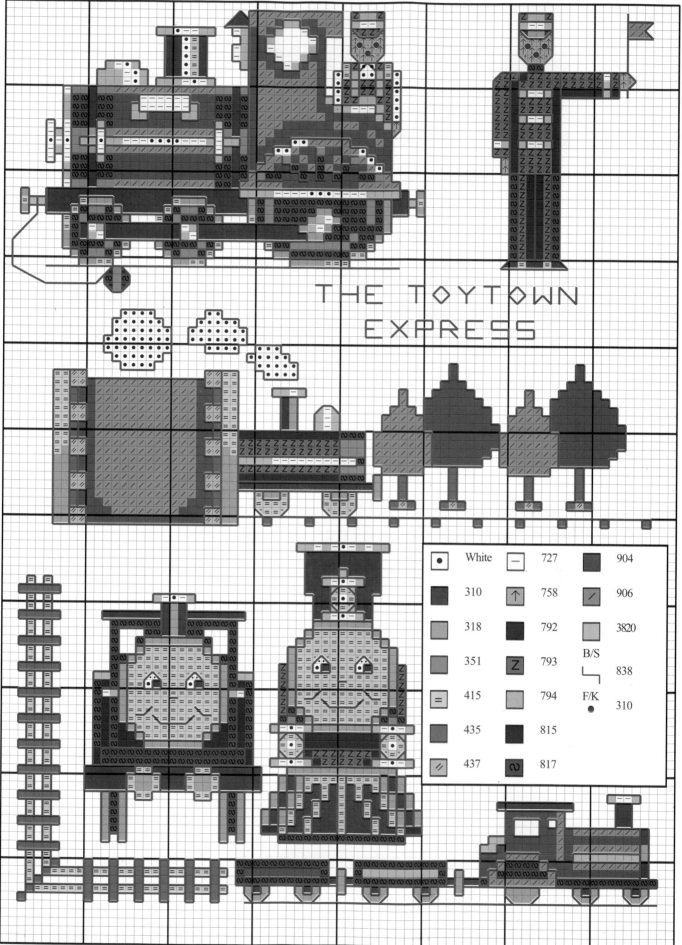

THE TOYTOWN
EXPRESS

	White	—	727		904
	310	↑	758	/	906
	318		792		3820
	351	Z	793		B/S
=	415		794	⌐	838
	435		815	F/K	
//	437	∽	817	•	310

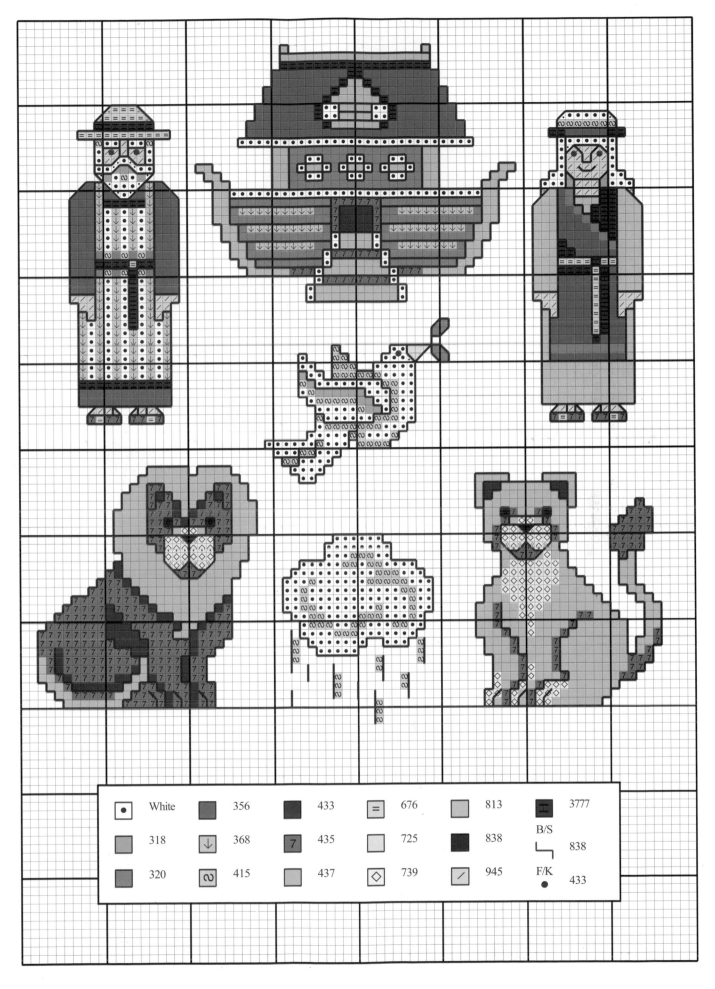

• White	356	433	= 676	813	⊥ 3777
318	↓ 368	7 435	725	838	B/S
320	∽ 415	437	◇ 739	/ 945	⌐ 838
					F/K ● 433

Yum Yum Mum

●	White		744	5	3712
2	334	8	758		3755
	415		760	B/S	
=	729		838	└	838
|	738	/	945		

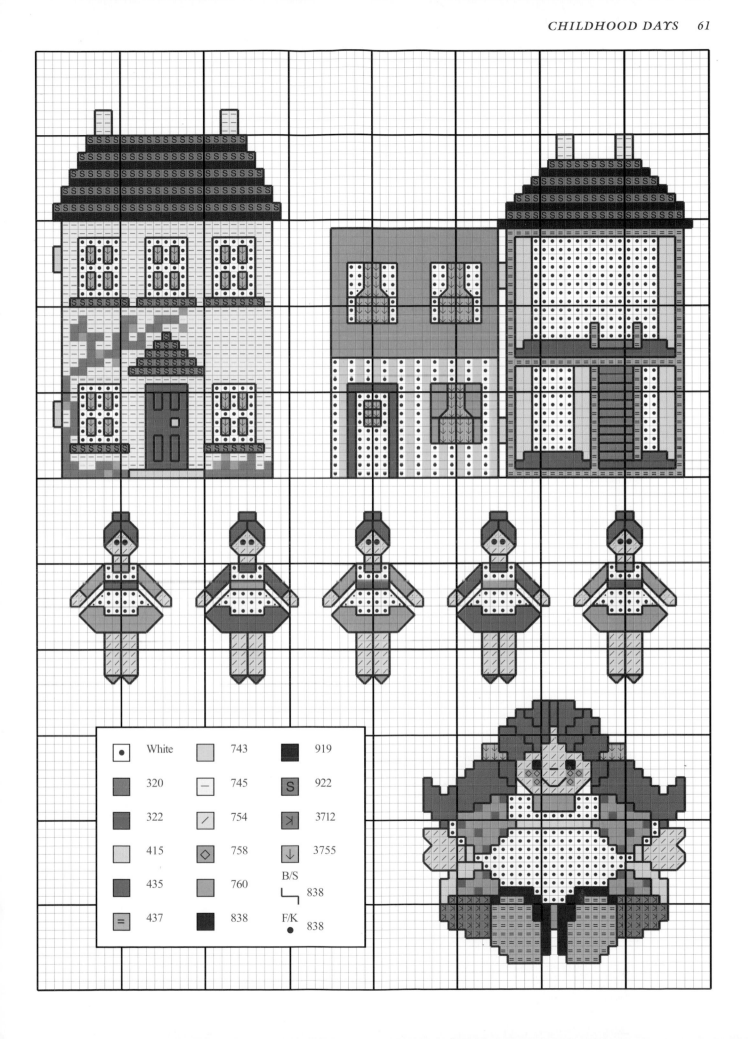

•	White	743	919
	320	— 745	S 922
	322	/ 754	3712
	415	◇ 758	↓ 3755
	435	760	B/S 838
=	437	838	F/K • 838

Favourite Things

Whether you enjoy munching chocolate, going on a shopping spree or walking the dog, you'll find something that appeals among these designs of favourite things. Celebrate your creativity by stitching designs inspired by dressmaking, quilting, knitting and, of course, cross stitch. Angels, antiques and bears are firm favourites with collectors so this chapter also includes charts so you can stitch a collector's cabinet full of treasured motifs.

Workbox Treasures

*Here's a practical way to show off your sewing skills by making a beautiful needlecase,
pin cushion and matching weight to keep track of your scissors.*

- ◆ **White 22-count Hardanger**
- ◆ **Contrasting felt**
- ◆ **Cord**
- ◆ **Small amount of filling**
- ◆ **Curtain weight**
- ◆ **Pinking shears**
- ◆ **Sewing equipment**

DESIGN NOTES

The design for these pretty sewing accessories is
taken from page 73 and you will see that I have
made some adaptations. Each design was sewn over
two threads on 22-count Hardanger using three
strands and I added a gold charm and a satin stitch
border. This was formed by making a series of
straight stitches using three strands over 4–5 blocks
of the aida. The completed stitching was fringed up
to the edge of this border.

MAKING THE NEEDLECASE, SCISSORS KEEPER AND PIN CUSHION

To make the needlecase, fringe the stitched design
and pin it to the edge of a square of felt leaving a
small amount of felt showing. Cut the felt wide
enough to fold in half form the back of the needlecase. Sew the design in place. Cut two further strips
of felt, slightly narrower and shorter than the outside of the case to make some pages. Pin the pages
and the needlecase cover together at the centre of
the case. Machine stitch through all these layers to
secure them to the needlecase. Fold some contrasting threads in half and twist them together to make
two short cords for tying the needlecase. Sew the
looped end of each one to opposite sides of the
needlecase and secure the loose ends with a knot.

To make the scissors keeper, fringe the design and
use it as a pattern to cut two pieces of felt, about
6mm (¼ in) larger all round. Sew your design to one
of these pieces of felt. Then with wrong sides facing,
pin it to the other piece of felt and join the sides
with a running stitch leaving the top open. Push in
a small amount of filling through this opening, then
the curtain weight and some more filling on top.
Twist together threads to make a cord and slip one
end into the opening. Close the opening with
running stitches, at the same time securing the cord.
Add a little clear glue to the other end of the cord
and knot your embroidery scissors to it. Make the
pin cushion in the same way, stuffing it firmly.

*I adapted motifs from page 70 to decorate the lid of a
sewing box. I stitched them on 22-count Hardanger and
added a straight stitch border using three strands.
The design was cut out with pinking shears, trimmed
with buttons and stuck to the lid of the box.*

Sewing Notions Wall Hanging

Make a pretty wall hanging covered with motifs on the theme of needlework to celebrate some of your own favourite things.

- ◆ **Selection of stitched designs**
- ◆ **Fabric for front of hanging**
- ◆ **Felt for backing**
- ◆ **Wadding (batting)**
- ◆ **Buttons, charms or other decorative items**
- ◆ **Small scraps of felt**
- ◆ **Iron-on adhesive**
- ◆ **D rings for hanging**
- ◆ **Sewing equipment**

DESIGN NOTES

This is another variation on the hangings that appear in other chapters. You will see that I added a single line of cross stitches around each of my chosen motifs to make a border. I attached each design to the background fabric with iron-on adhesive.

MAKING THE WALL HANGING

1 Lay out your stitched pieces on the background fabric and decide where they should be positioned on the hanging. Decide how much print fabric should be visible between each one, referring to the photograph on page 62 if you need to. You can now work out how much fabric to cut for the quilt front. Add an extra 6 mm (¼ in) all round for joining it to the felt backing.

2 Trim each stitched piece 7–10 squares outside the single-stitch border. Using an iron-on adhesive and following the manufacturer's instructions carefully, stick your stitched pieces to the right side of the print fabric. Use this as a pattern to cut your felt backing and wadding (batting), making these slightly smaller than the main fabric.

3 Tack (baste) the wadding (batting) to the wrong side of the fabric. Attach the charms and buttons by stitching them through these layers and pulling the thread quite tightly to give a quilted look. The decorative buttons can be sewn on top of a small square of felt trimmed with pinking shears to make them stand out more.

4 Position the D rings on one side of the felt and sew them securely in place. Pin the felt to the back of the quilted piece and turn and press the zig zag edges on the print fabric to the back. Pin and neatly slipstitch in place.

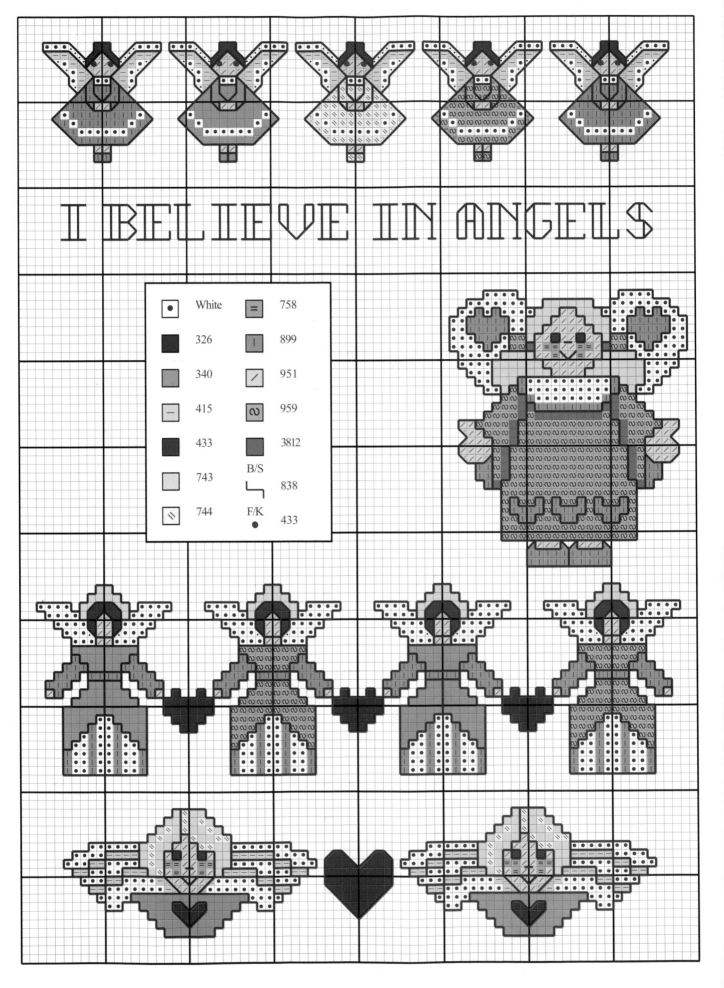

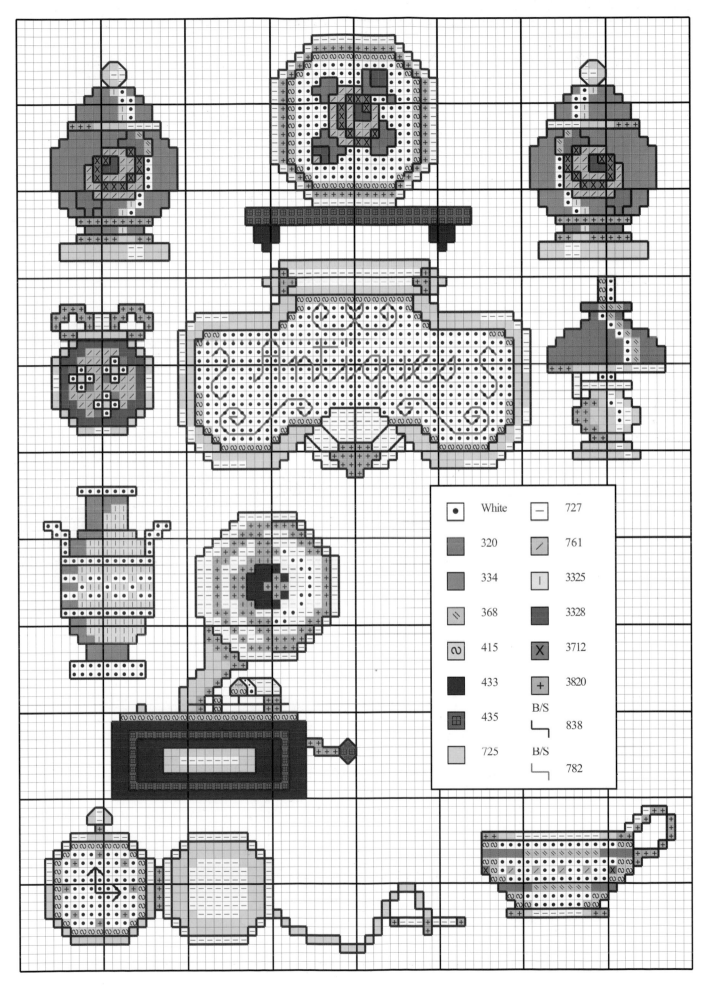

●	White	—	727
	320	/	761
	334	I	3325
	368		3328
∾	415	X	3712
	433	+	3820
⊞	435	B/S ⌐	838
	725	B/S ⌐	782

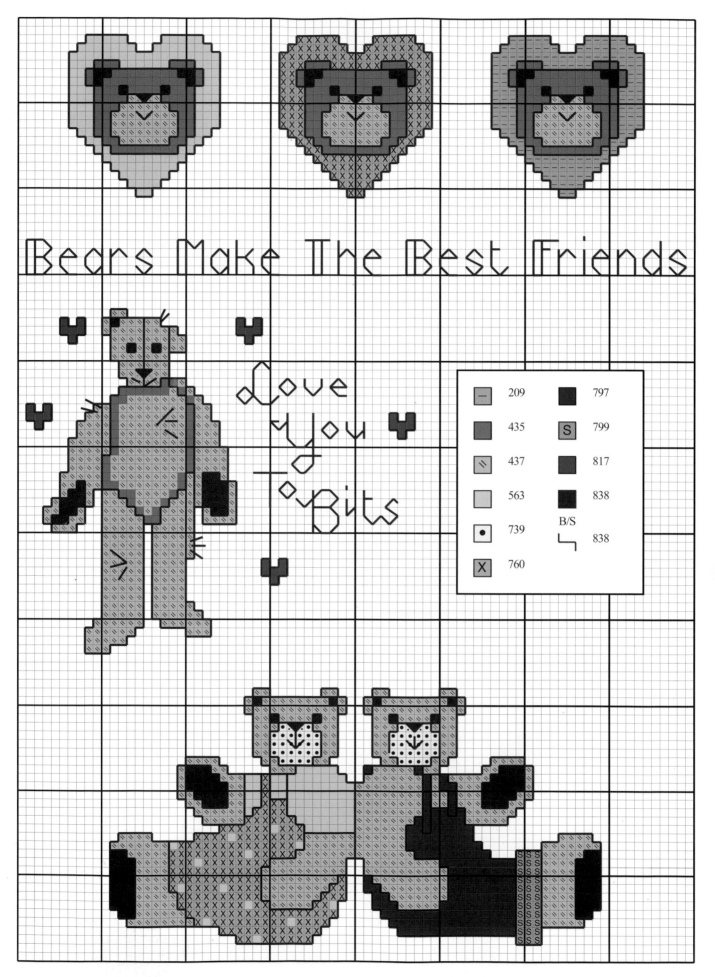

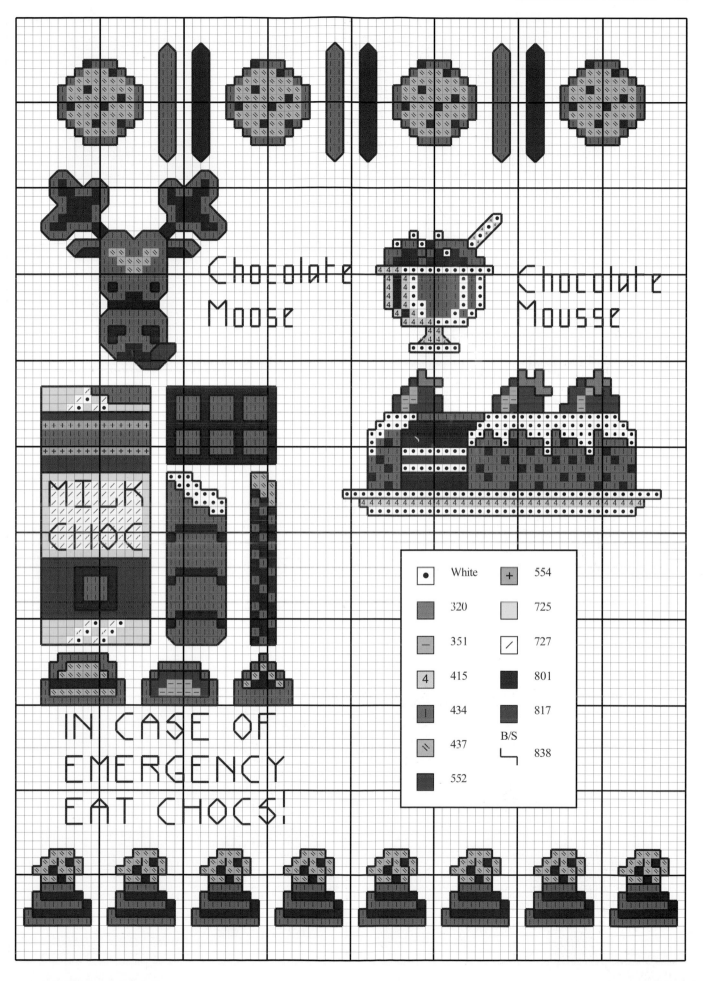

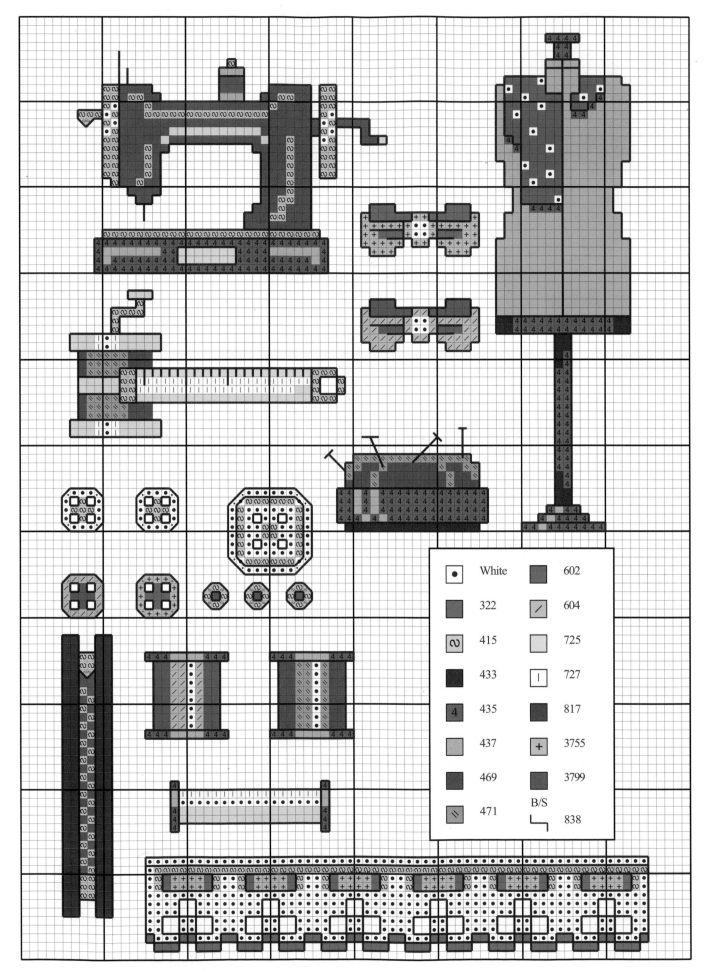

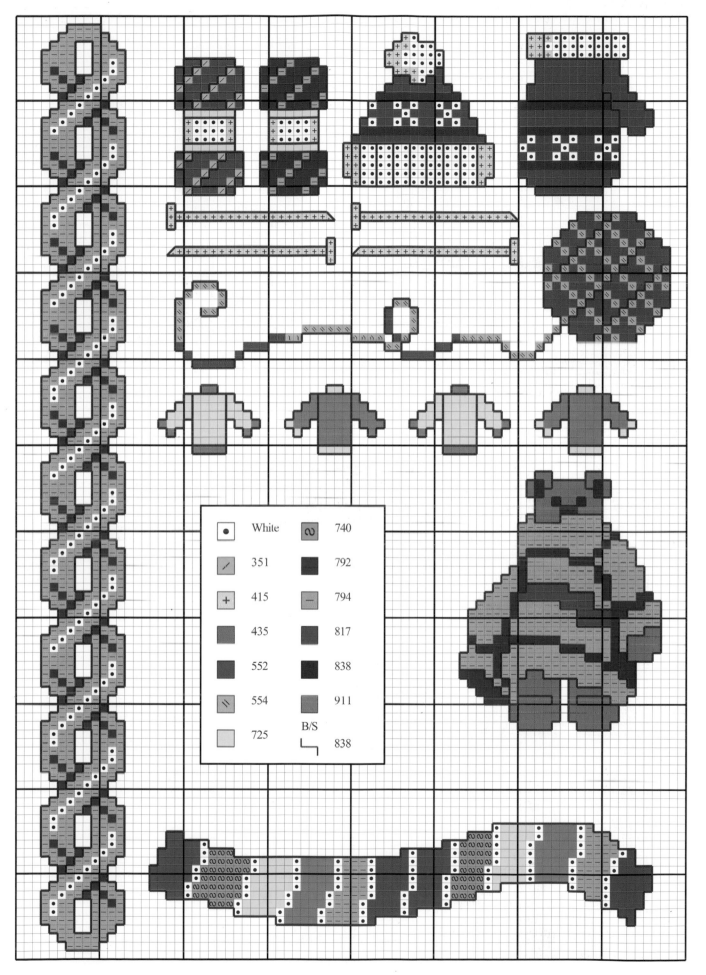

	White	∾	740
∕	351		792
+	415	—	794
	435		817
	552		838
∕∕	554		911
	725	B/S	
		⌐	838

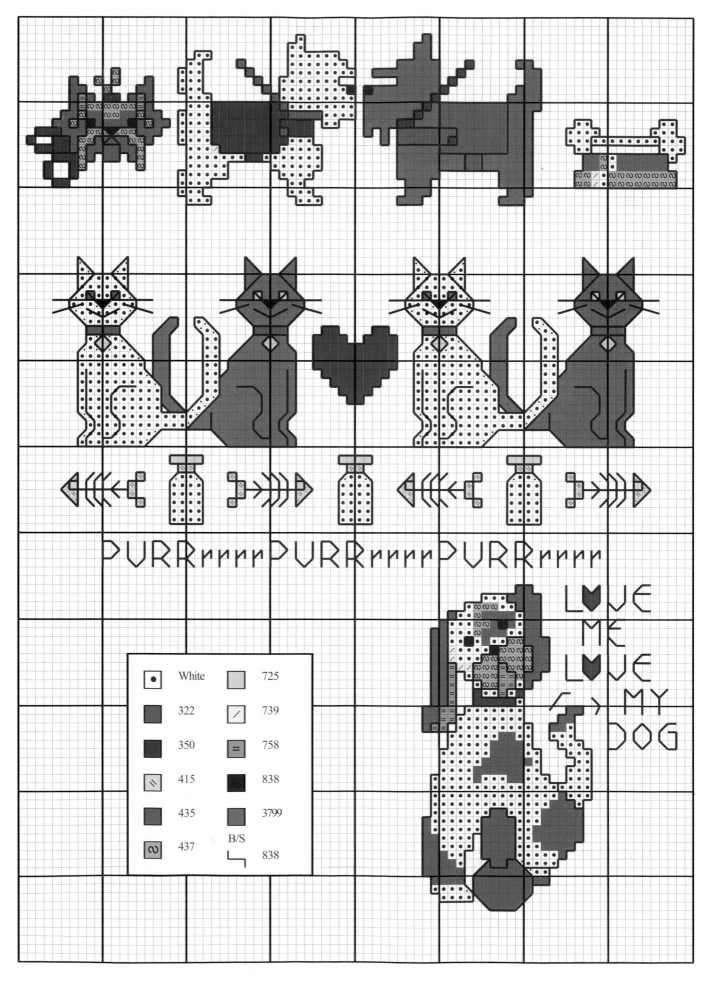

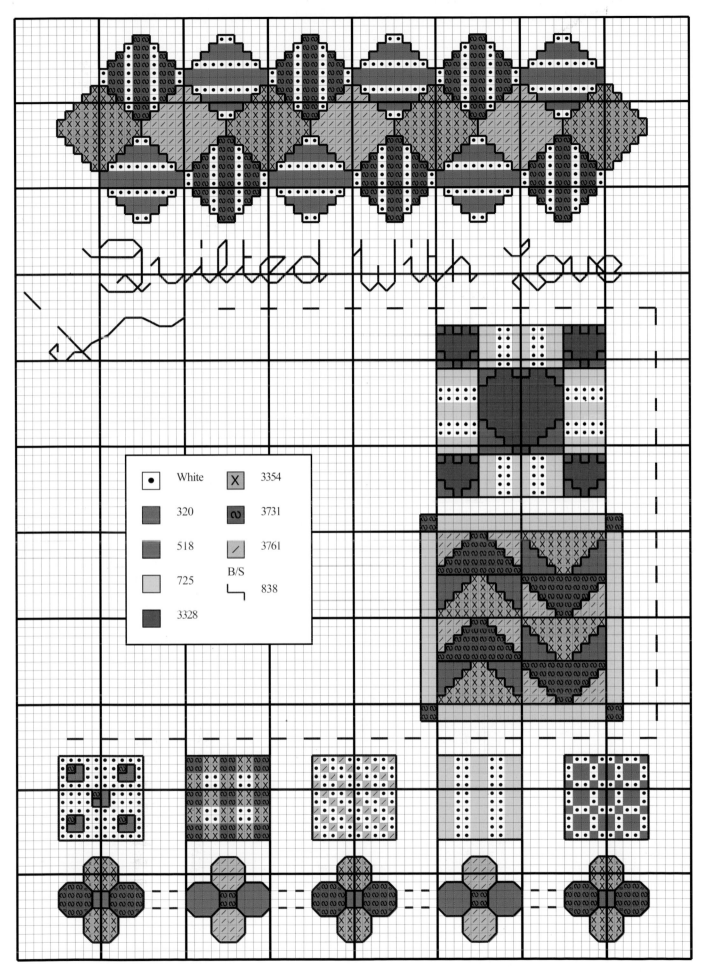

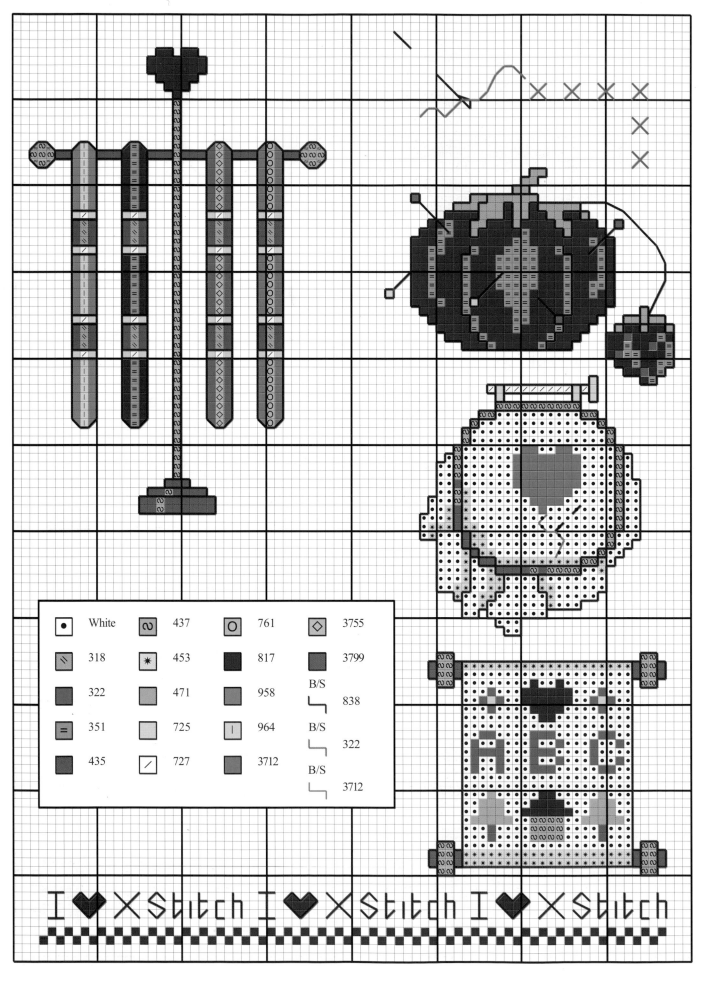

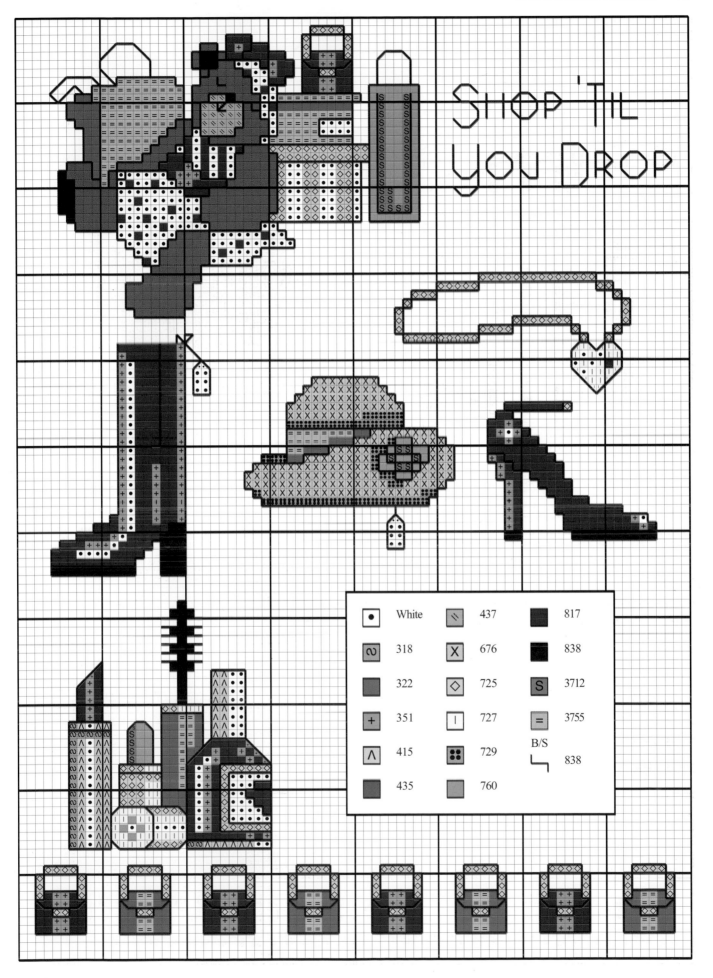

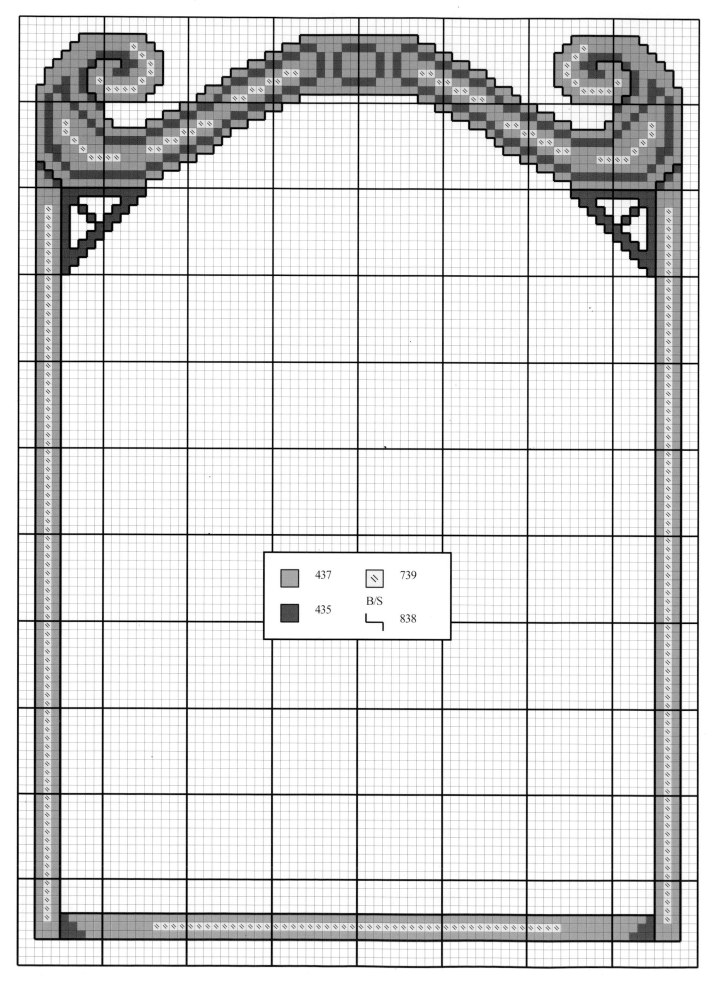

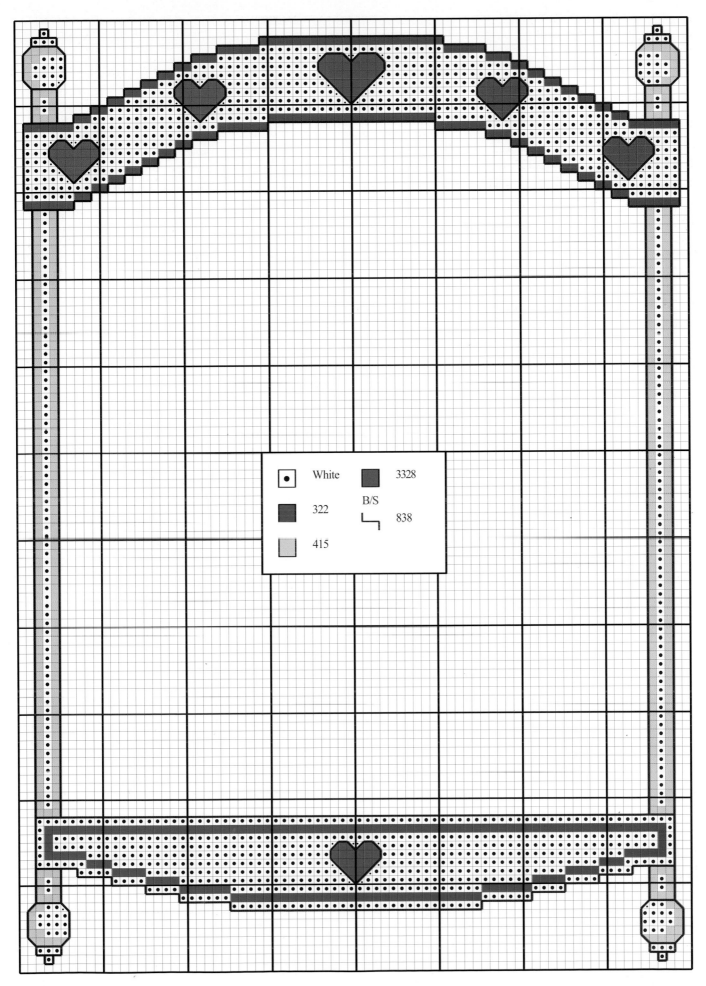

Holiday Memories

Do you dream of dipping your toes in a crystal clear ocean? Or are you more likely to be found enjoying a donkey ride before you eat fish and chips on the pier? Whatever your holiday destination, if you're a keen stitcher there's always room in your luggage for some stitching. These holiday motifs are ideal for taking away with you. Now you can stitch a lasting reminder of a lovely time to go with the holiday snaps.

Memory Board

A memory board is a lovely way to display treasured pieces of stitching and other reminders of a good holiday. I used an ordinary cork noticeboard as the basis for my board.

- **Stitched motifs**
- **Cork noticeboard**
- **Brightly-coloured felt**
- **PVA glue**
- **Trimmings (such as rope, cord etc)**
- **Decorative items (shells, charms, starfish etc)**

DESIGN NOTES

You can cover your noticeboard with felt or a print fabric using a small amount of PVA glue, or, as I did, leave the cork visible. I chose designs on the theme of seaside holidays. I stitched the four light-houses from page 82, treated them with Needlework Finisher (see page 11) and stuck them to brightly-coloured pieces of felt cut into the shape of signal pennants. I glued these to a length of string. I also stitched the pier, donkey and fishing boat motifs from page 83–4 and added a single line of contrasting stitches around each one to form a border. By cutting round each one just outside this border with pinking shears, I made them look rather like postcards. You can have a lot of fun finding your own ways of displaying your holiday motifs.

Holiday Album & Stitched Postcards

Here's a lovely gift to make for a friend who's off on their travels—an album decorated with your own stitched design to hold all the memories of their trip. Or you can use the holiday motifs in this chapter to stitch a series of postcards—they're ideal for taking with you when you go away.

- **Stitched motifs**
- **Small notebook or photo album**
- **Cards (without apertures)**
- **Glue**

OPPOSITE:
This Weather sampler was created from the motifs charted on pages 92–3. These were arranged in a balanced and symmetrical way with the four little seasons pictures providing a strong base line across the bottom. Turn to page 8 if you need more hints on how to create your own sampler using the charts in this book. A double mount sets off the whole design beautifully.

DESIGN NOTES

I turned the palm tree design and the wording on page 89 into a label for the front of my album. I stitched this quick design on perforated paper in colours to complement the album cover.

The cruise ship card was stitched on pale-blue 14-count aida and I gave it a simple red and blue border rather like an air-mail envelope. I cut round the design with pinking shears and stuck it to the front of a card. The Hawaiian Ted was stitched over two threads on 22-count Hardanger, stiffened with Needlework Finisher (see page 11), cut to shape and stuck on to a tropical coloured card.

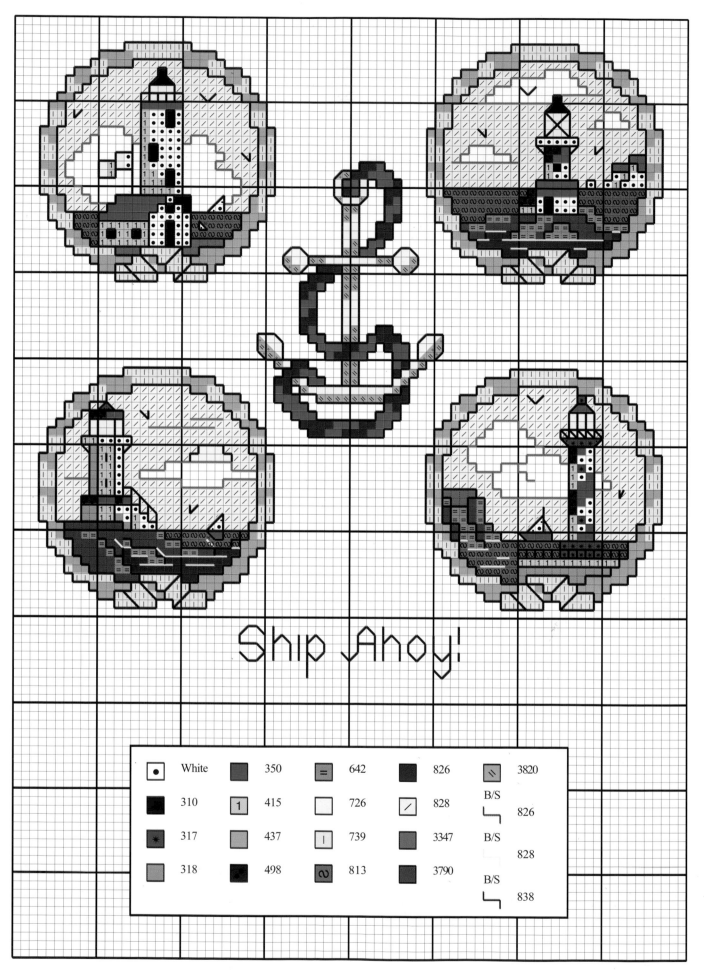

	White		350		642		826		3820
	310	1	415		726	/	828	B/S	826
	317		437		739		3347	B/S	828
	318		498	2	813		3790	B/S	838

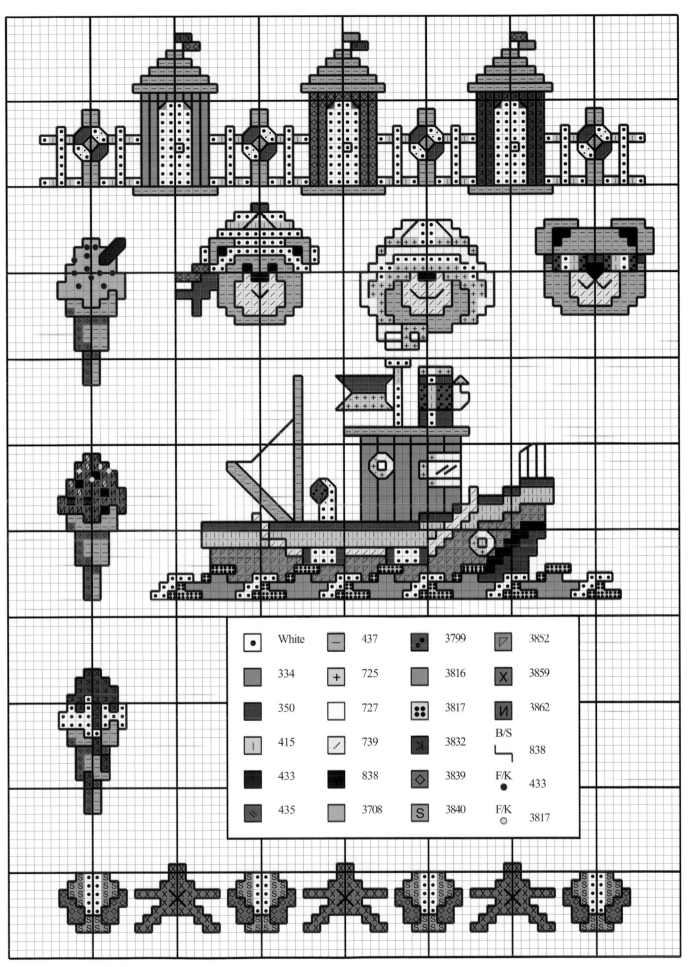

	White		437		3799		3852
	334	+	725		3816	X	3859
	350		727		3817	Иꞁ	3862
	415	/	739		3832	**B/S**	
	433		838		3839		838
	435		3708	S	3840	**F/K**	433
						F/K	3817

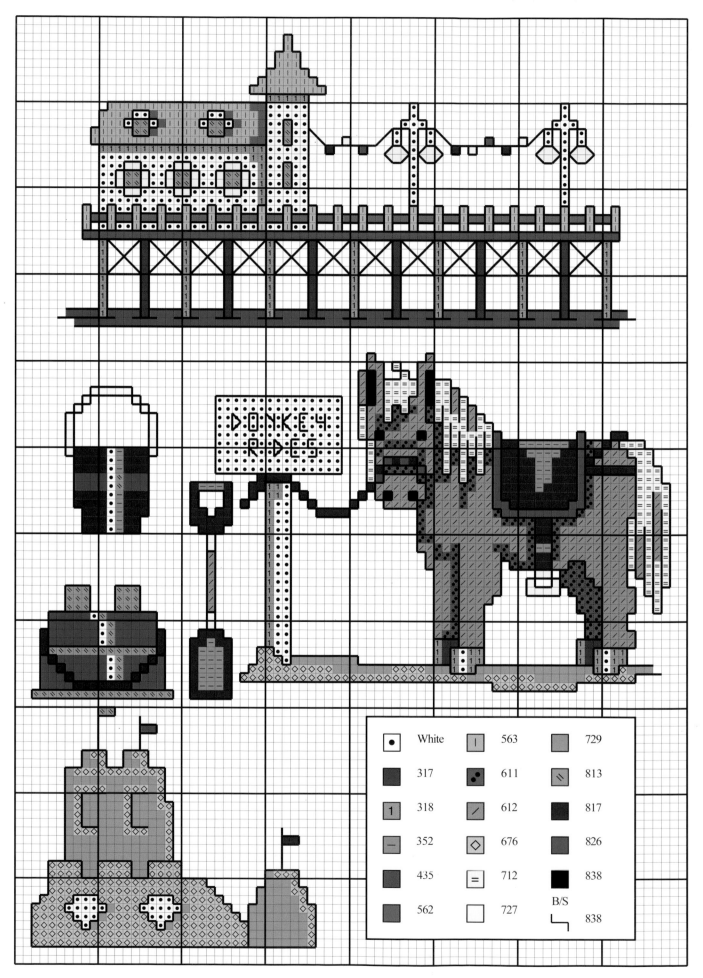

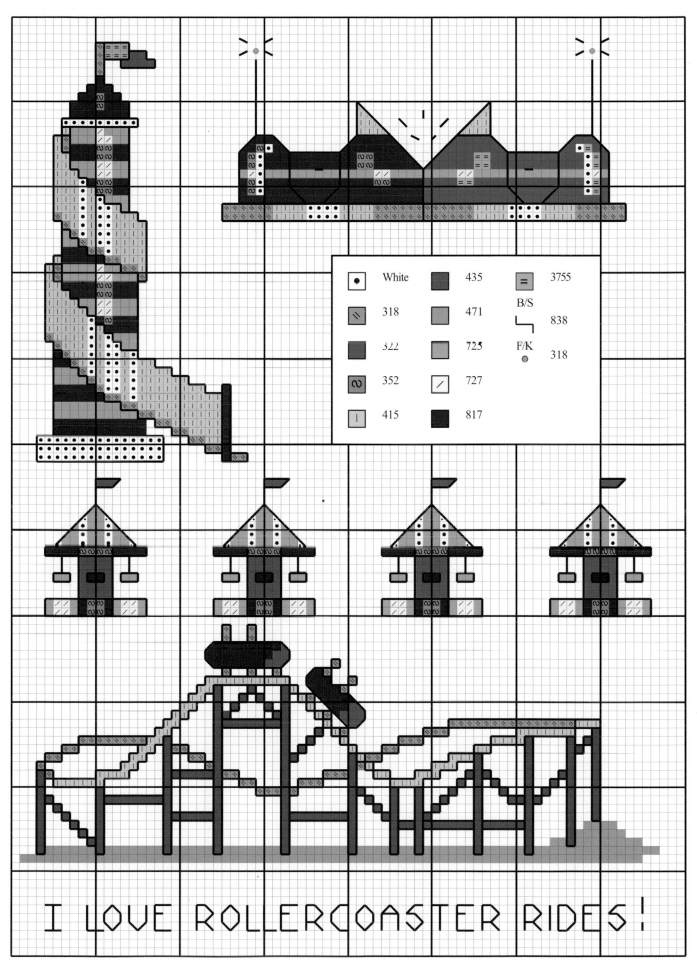

	White		435			=	3755
	318		471		B/S	└─┘	838
	322		725		F/K	●	318
	352		727				
	415		817				

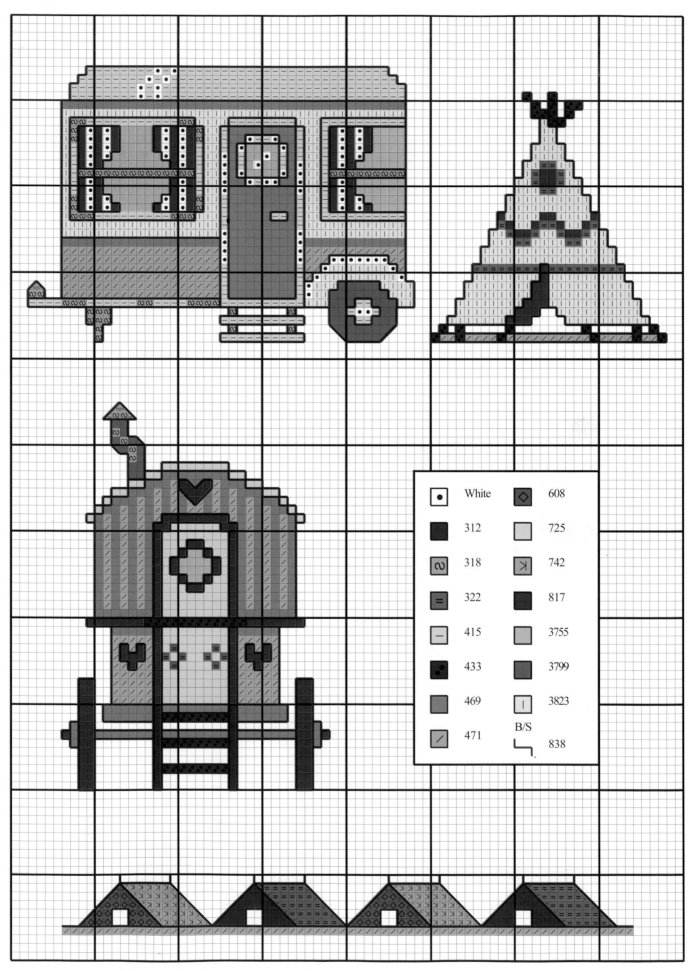

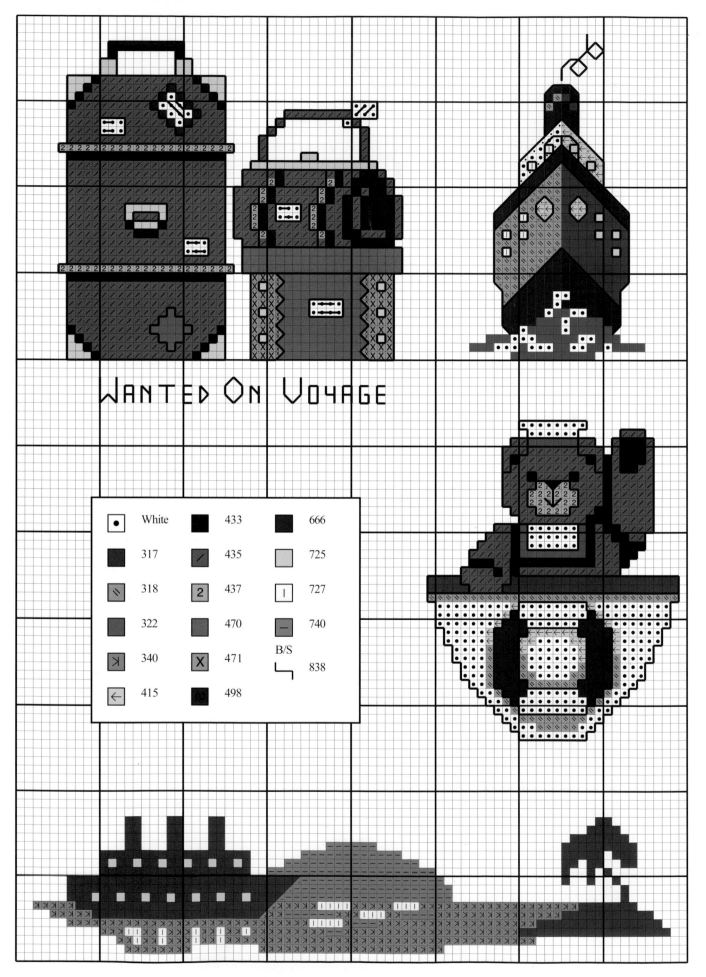

WANTED ON VOYAGE

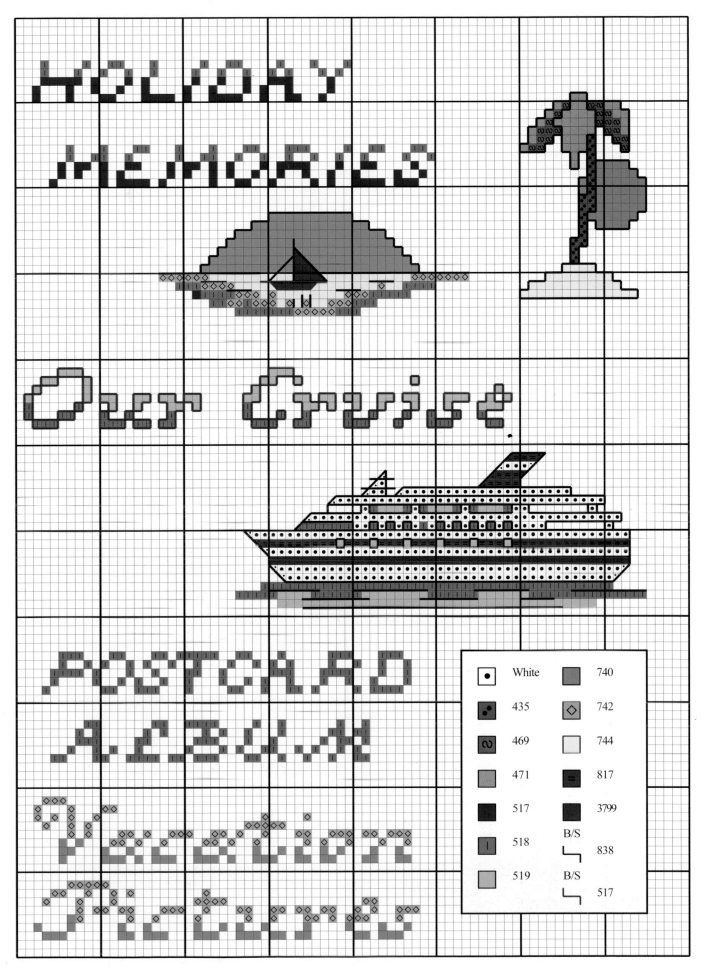

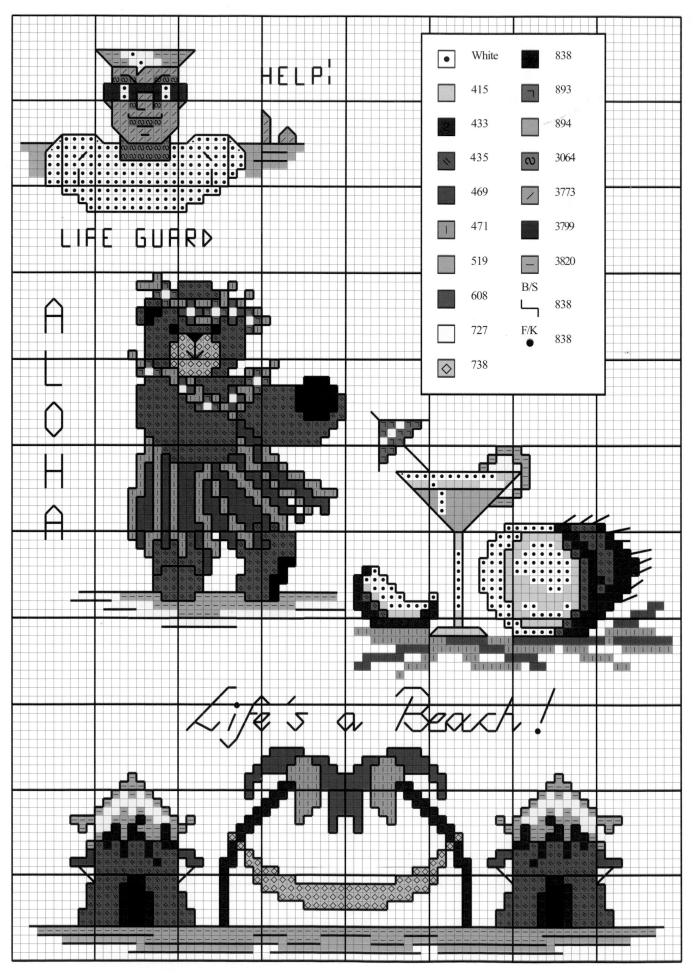

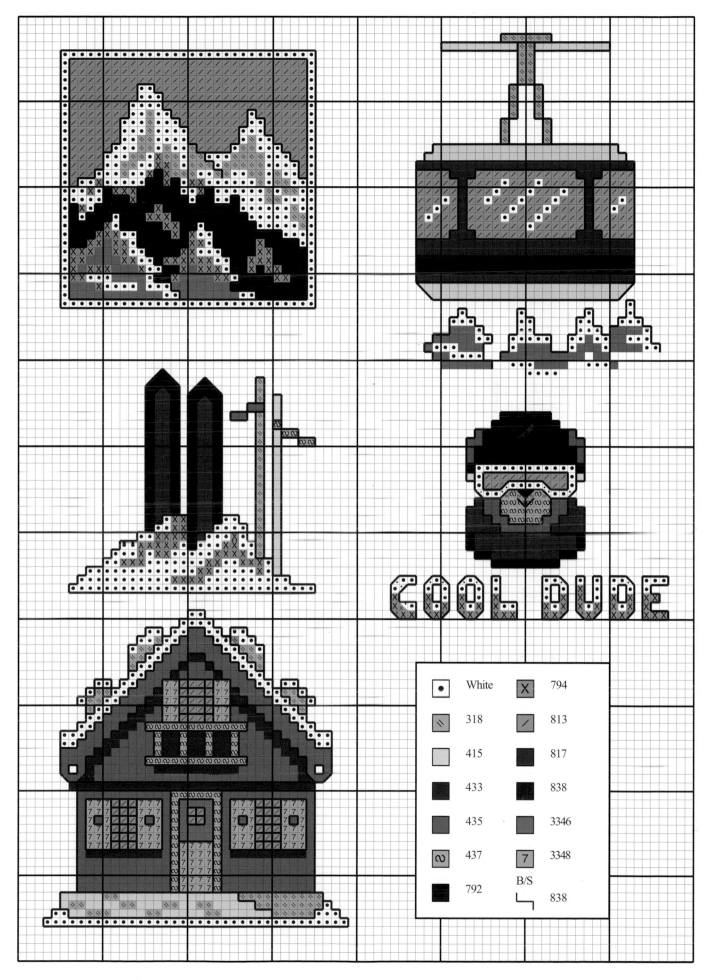

	White		794
	318		813
	415		817
	433		838
	435		3346
2	437	7	3348
	792	B/S	838

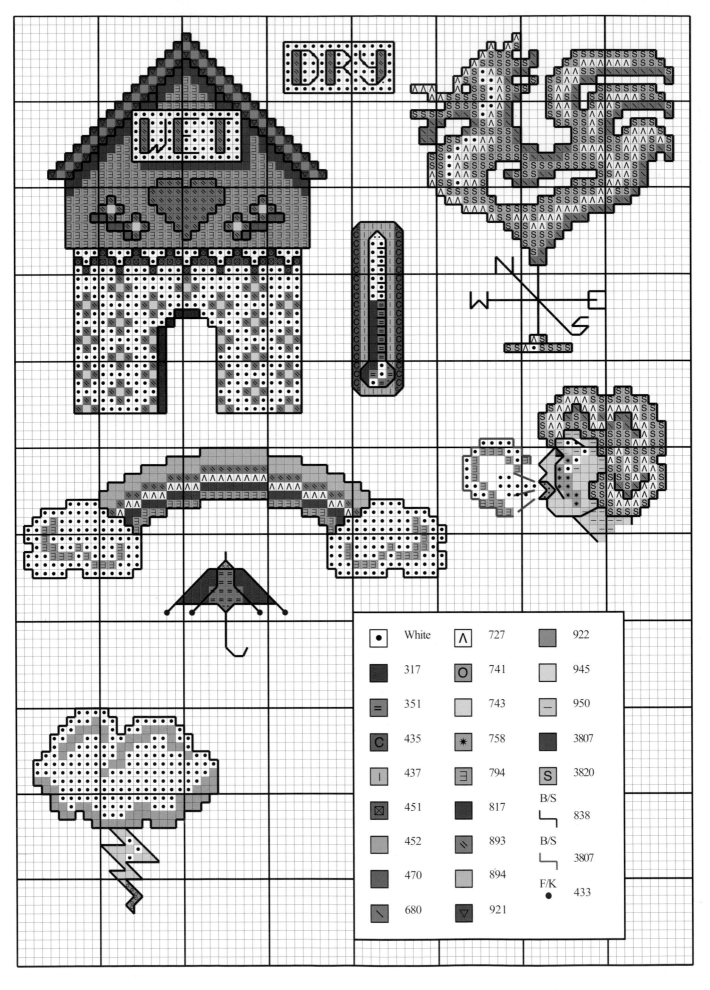

⊡	White	∧	727	▧	922
■	317	Ⓞ	741	▧	945
=	351	▨	743	−	950
C	435	✳	758	▧	3807
I	437	Ⅎ	794	S	3820
⊠	451	■	817	B/S	
▨	452	⁄⁄	893	⌐	838
▨	470	▨	894	B/S	
＼	680	▽	921	⌐	3807
				F/K	
				●	433

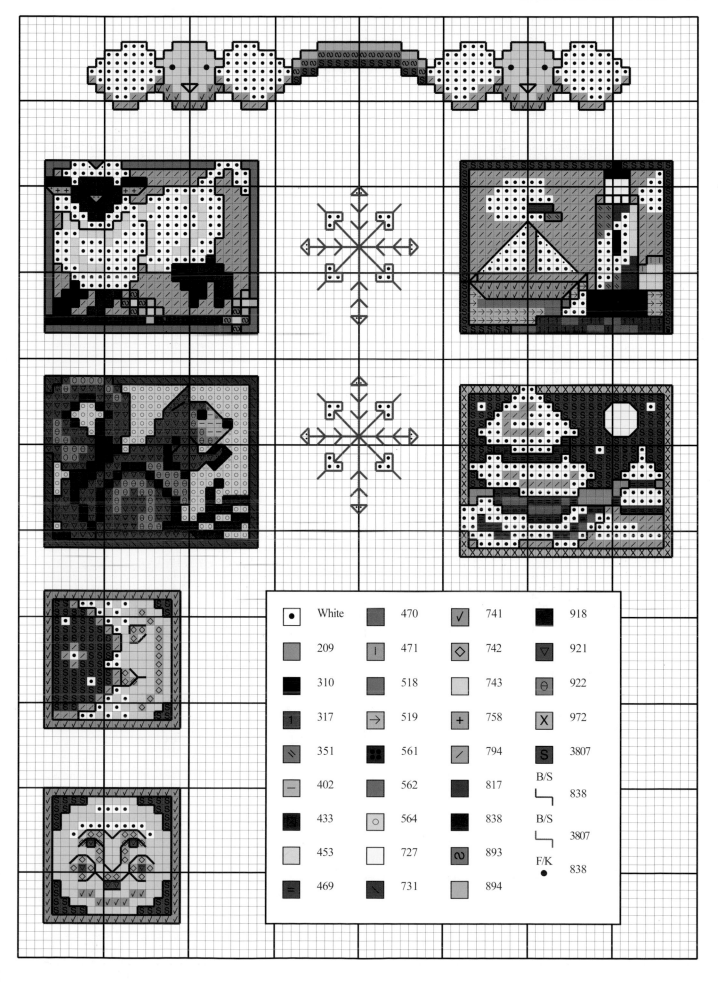

●	White		470	✓	741		918			
	209	I	471	◇	742	▽	921			
	310		518		743	θ	922			
1	317	→	519	+	758	X	972			
∕∕	351		561	∕	794	S	3807			
—	402		562		817	B/S	838			
	433	○	564		838	B/S	3807			
	453		727	2	893	F/K				
=	469	╲	731		894	●	838			

Once upon a
time . . . . .
at the end of the
rainbow . . .

in a splendid big
castle . . .

there lived
a brave
young
knight
who was
called –

STEPHEN

Land of Dreams

'Once upon a time'... these are the words that unlock the door to magical realms of fantasy and adventure. Now you can write your own story in stitches by choosing from the fairytale characters in this chapter. A fairy godmother, the frog prince, a spell-binding wizard and a genie awaiting your commands – you'll find them all here. Use them to stitch delightful projects for children, or for grown-ups who are still young at heart.

Brave Knight Wall Hanging

Make a wall hanging by combining some of the fantasy charts on the following pages vertically rather than horizontally. The result is a wonderful shield hanging every young prince will want for their bedroom wall.

- ◆ **Cream 14-count aida fabric**
- ◆ **Felt for backing**
- ◆ **Felt scraps for the shield**
- ◆ **Clear glue**
- ◆ **Paper to make a pattern**
- ◆ **Graph paper and drawing equipment**
- ◆ **Scissors and sewing equipment**
- ◆ **Two D rings for hanging**

DESIGN NOTES

Turn to pages 6–9 for advice on how to chart your master design. I used the following motifs from this chapter on my hanging: The 'Once upon a time...' lettering, the knight and shields on page 98; the rainbow with the pot of gold and the castle on pages 105 and 99. The lettering was charted from the alphabet on page 126. As a rule, stitched lettering looks better than backstitch out-

lining and is easier to read if stitched in a medium to dark shade. Outlining solid letters is a matter of personal choice.

MAKING THE WALL HANGING

1 Allow enough fabric all round the design for the size of your banner and add an extra 12 mm (1 in) seam allowance. Turn this seam allowance to the wrong side of your completed stitching and press firmly in place. Make sure that the edges are straight, especially if the design is as long as this one, because these will be used as a guide to attach the stitched piece to the backing.

2 Calculate the size for the backing by measuring the length and width of your neatened stitching. Felt is the best fabric for this because it doesn't fray and does not require any stitching. Decide how much felt you want to show around the edge of the design and whether to shape the bottom edge as I did. When you have calculated the size and shape of your backing, draw a paper pattern (use greaseproof from a roll if you need to cut a large shape). Pin this to the felt and cut out using sharp, long-bladed dressmaking scissors.

3 It is easier to position the D rings and stitch them in place at the back of the felt before attaching the stitched piece to the backing. Now carefully pin your stitched piece to the front of the felt. Tack (baste) it in place to ensure it is straight. Machine or slipstitch as close to the folded edge of the aida as possible. If you want to make a shield, draw the shape onto a piece of card, cut this out and cover with scraps of felt.

The Princess in the Tower Wall Hanging

Here's a fun and creative way to use your stitching. Make a castle for a child's room and fill it with stitched figures of a dragon, a knight and a princess. I hope my castle will inspire you to make a really special project that will be treasured for many years.

- ◆ **Cream 14-count aida**
- ◆ **Velcro strip – hooked part only**
- ◆ **Large piece of paper for castle pattern (graph paper is ideal)**
- ◆ **Very stiff interfacing (used for tailored lapels) or good quality card for the castle backing**
- ◆ **Large piece of felt for the castle walls**
- ◆ **Dark brown felt for the door and balcony; light brown felt for the tower roof; grey felt for the stonework; green felt for the grass; pale blue felt for the windows**
- ◆ **Scraps of felt for heraldic shields**
- ◆ **Eight brass paper fasteners**
- ◆ **Pencil, ruler, black fine felt tip pen**
- ◆ **Double-sided tape**
- ◆ **Clear glue**
- ◆ **Sewing equipment**
- ◆ **Four D rings**

1 Stitch your figures first because they will determine the scale of your castle. Stiffen them with Needlework Finisher (see page 11) and cut out round each one close to the stitching line. Glue the hooked part of a Velcro strip to the back of each figure for attaching it to the felt.

2 Draw a pattern for your castle on 10 squares to the inch graph paper. Keep the shape as simple as possible – make the main part of the castle and tower all one piece. Next, cut this base shape from very stiff interfacing or card. Then use it as a pattern to cut the main walls from the felt. Add details such as window arches at this stage with a running stitch. Cover the base with strips of double-sided tape and attach the felt. Lastly, neaten the edges by applying clear glue if necessary.

3 Cut a roof for the tower out of light brown felt and add some chain stitch detail as I did if preferred. Cut another, smaller piece of felt for the portcullis and add stonework by cutting out grey felt and stitching it to the edges. Use blue felt for the windows, stitching any details before attaching them. The castle door is simply a piece of brown felt with brass paper fasteners pushed through it to give the effect of heavy studding. Use a pair of sharp scissors to cut out a balcony shape from dark brown felt. If you want to stand a figure on it, stitch it in place only on three sides to form a pocket. Cut spiky strips of green felt for the grass. Use any brightly coloured felt scraps to make the shields and glue in place.

4 Stitch the four D rings in a line across the back of the hanging.

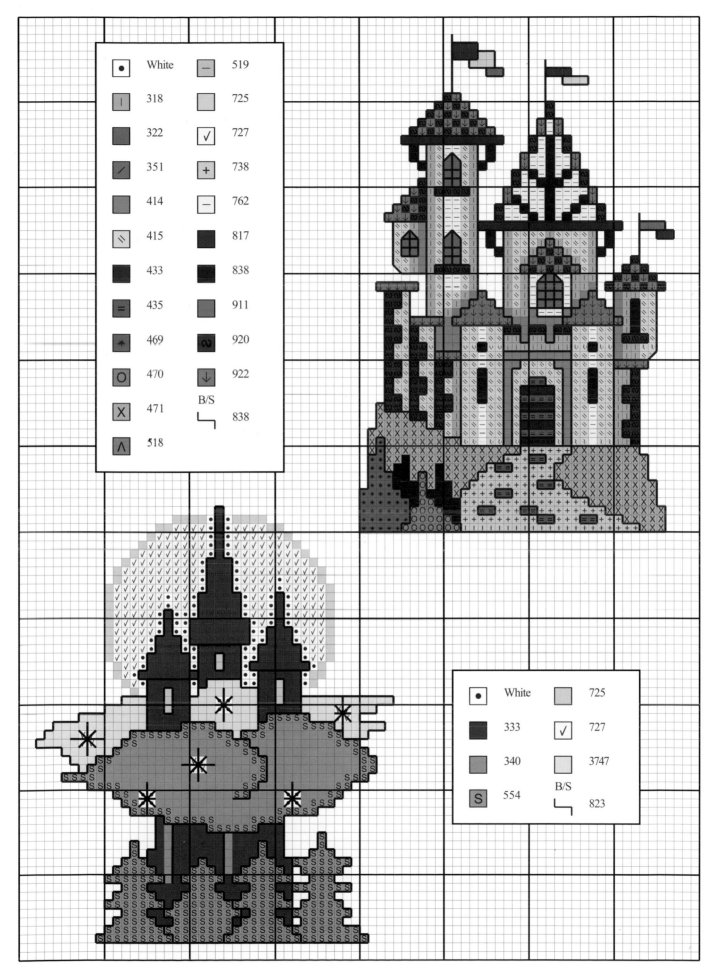

●	White	▬	519
▮	318	▢	725
▮	322	✓	727
╱	351	+	738
▮	414	—	762
╲╲	415	▮	817
▮	433	▮	838
=	435	▮	911
✱	469	∽	920
O	470	↓	922
X	471	B/S	
∧	518	⌐	838

●	White	▢	725
▮	333	✓	727
▮	340	▢	3747
S	554	B/S	
		⌐	823

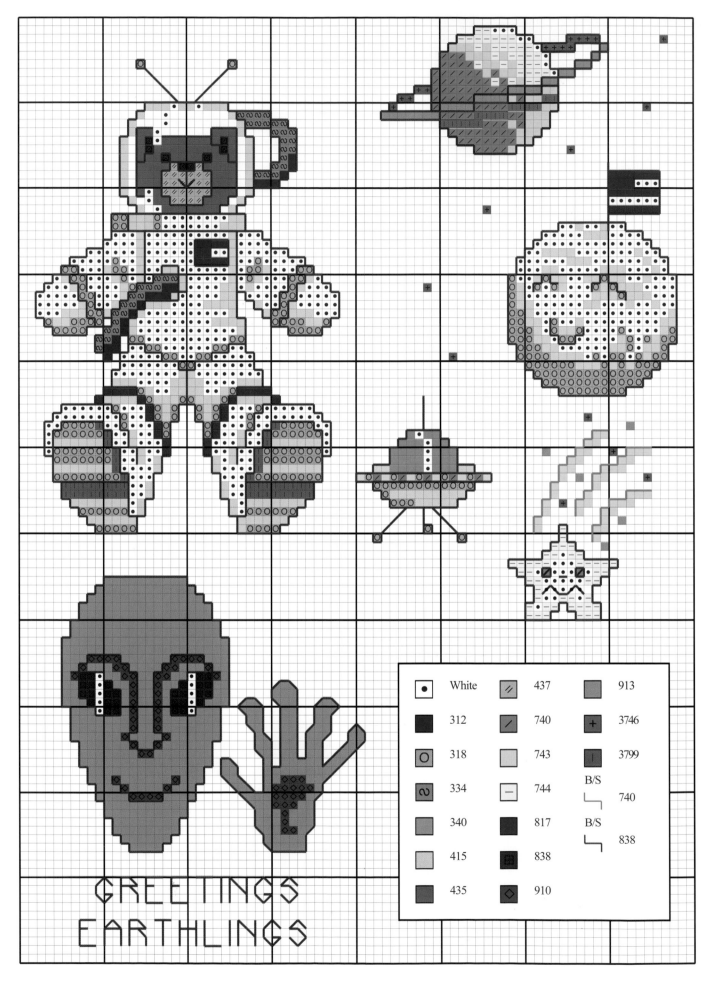

GREETINGS
EARTHLINGS

	White		437		913
	312		740	+	3746
	318		743		3799
	334		744	B/S	
	340		817		740
	415		838	B/S	
	435		910		838

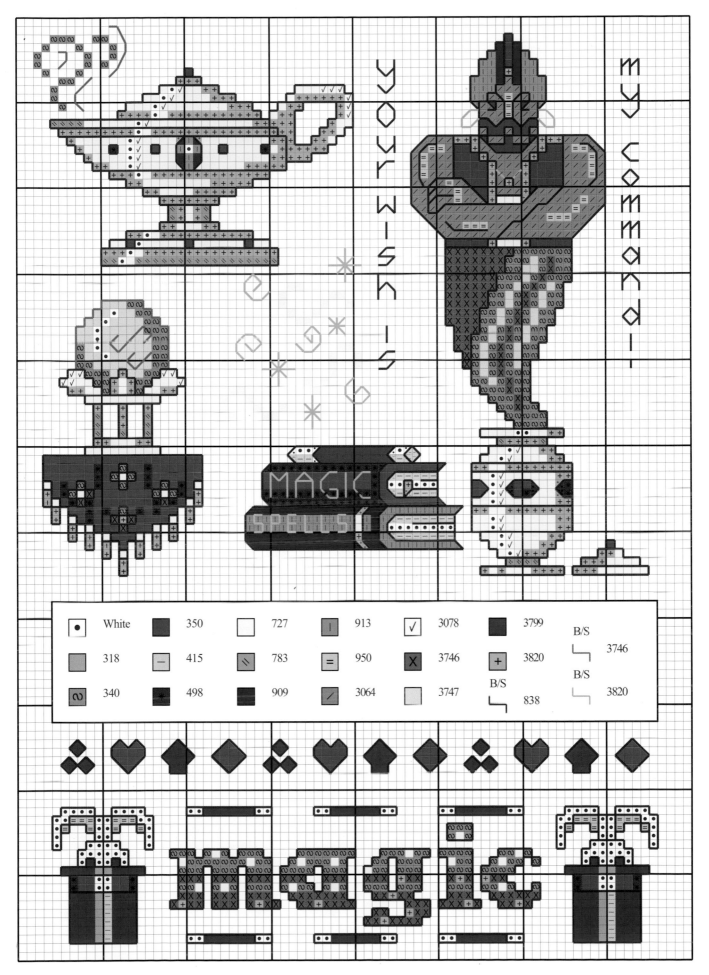

•	White		350		727		913	√	3078		3799
	318	—	415	∥	783	=	950	X	3746	+	3820
⌇	340		498		909	/	3064		3747		

B/S 3746

B/S 838

B/S 3820

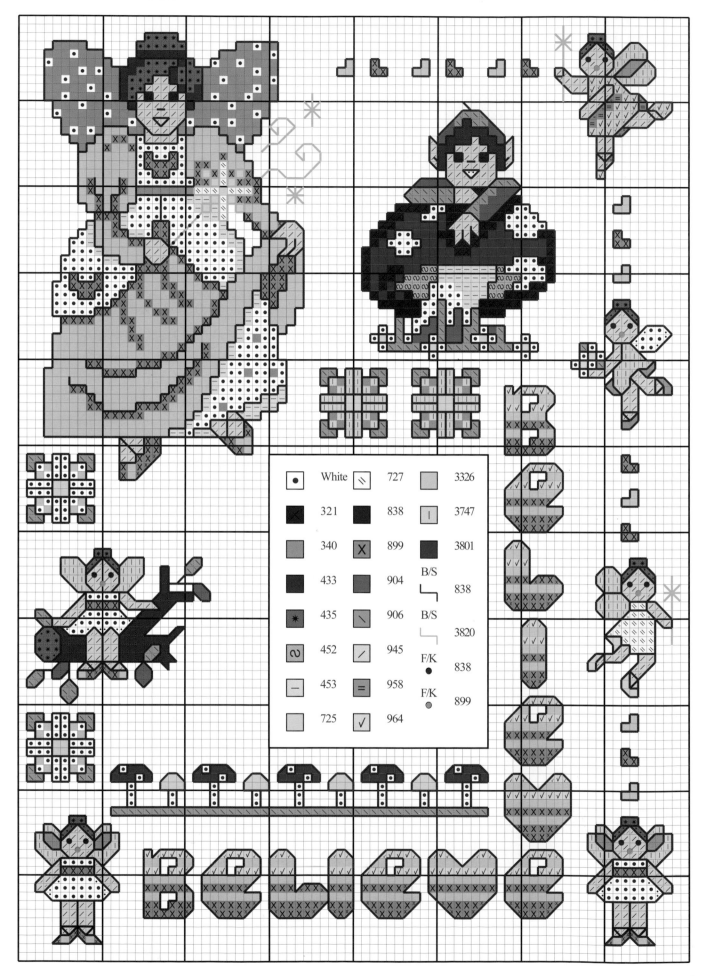

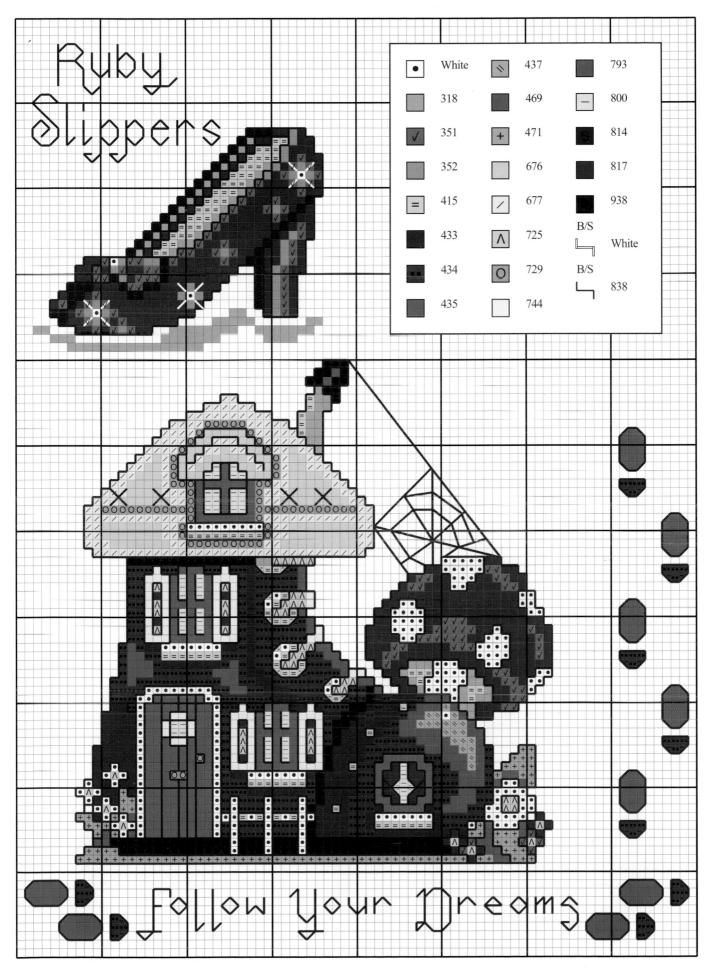

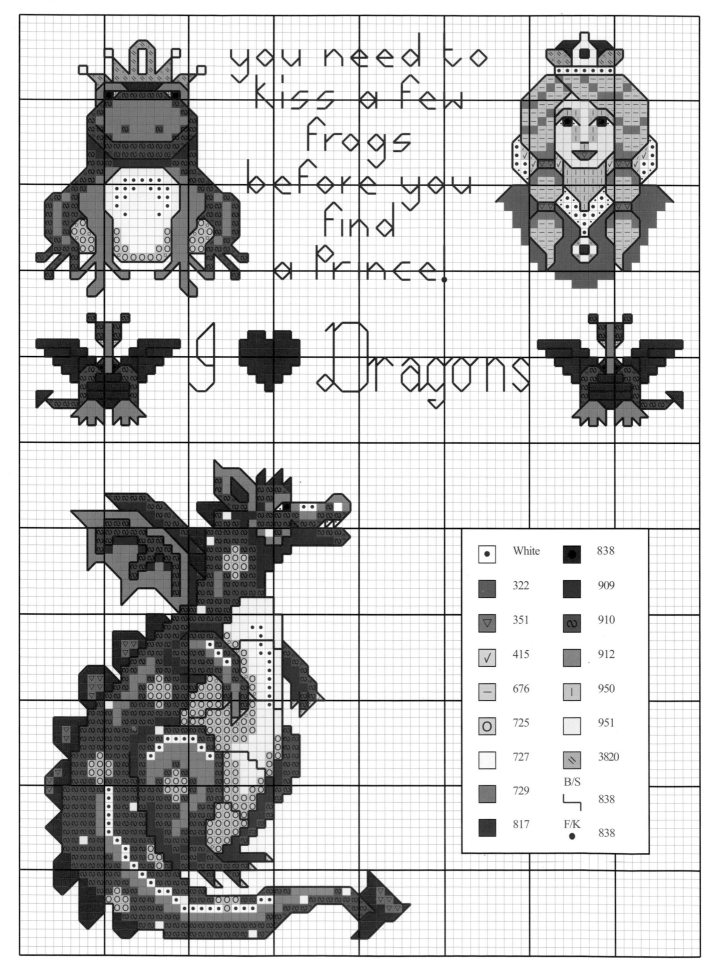

you need to kiss a few frogs before you find a Prince.

I ♥ Dragons

	White		838
	322		909
▽	351	∞	910
✓	415		912
–	676	I	950
O	725		951
	727	∖∖	3820
	729	B/S	
	817	⌐	838
		F/K	
		•	838

Hubble
Bubble!

☐	White	⬈ 742	
▬	340	754	
∿	415	⁄ 758	
■	433	3746	
=	676	3799	
	704	B/S 704	
	725	B/S 3799	
✕	740		

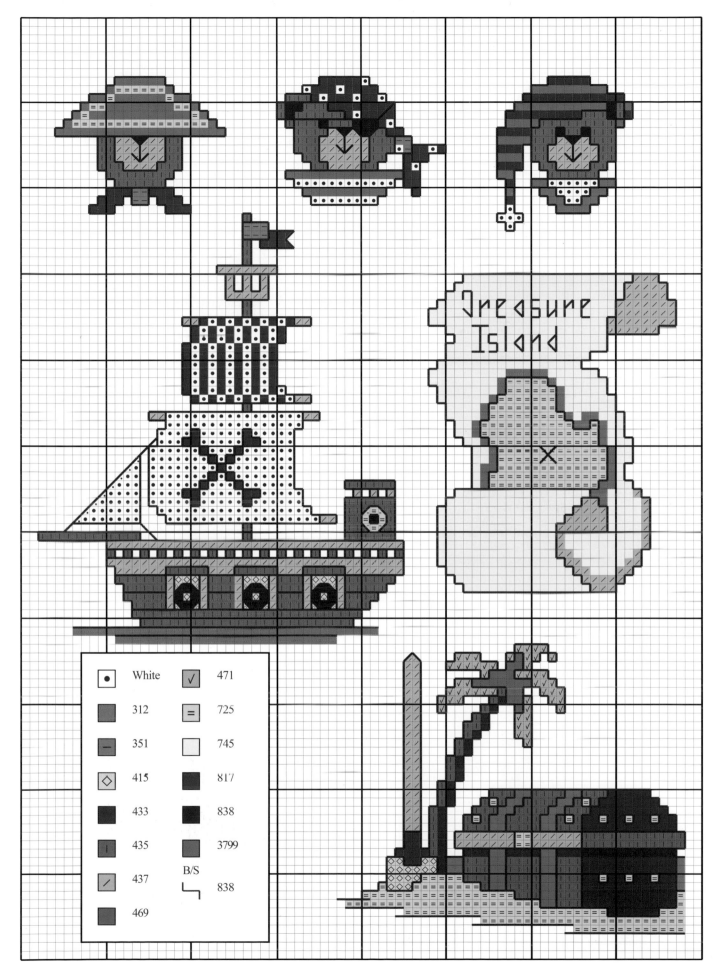

Treasure Island

	White		471
	312		725
	351		745
	415		817
	433		838
	435		3799
	437	B/S	
	469		838

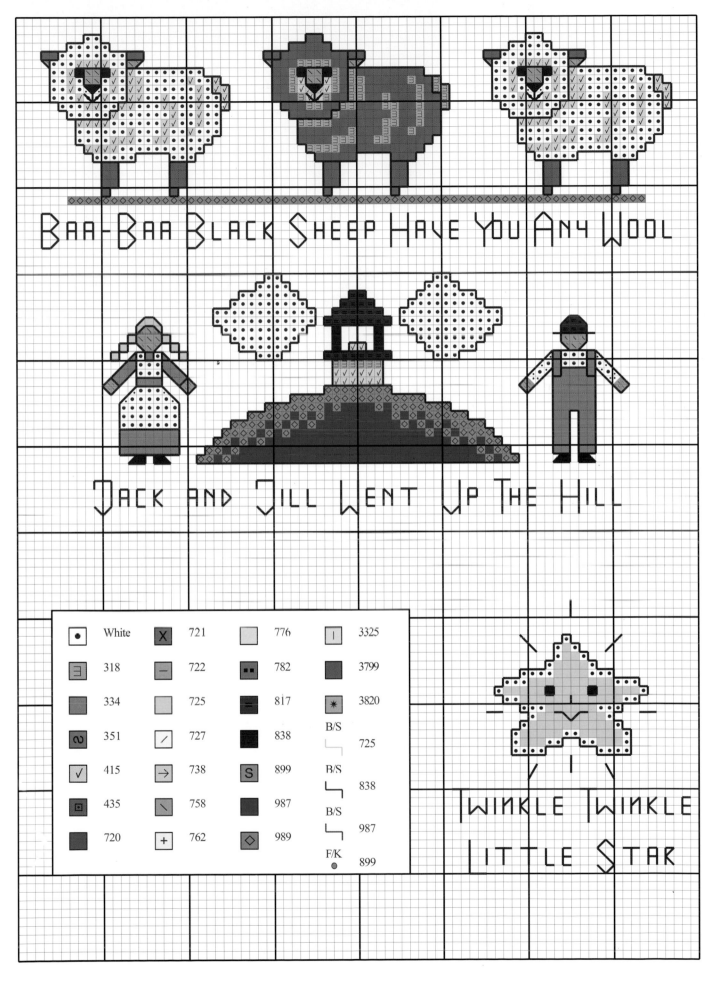

BAA-BAA BLACK SHEEP HAVE YOU ANY WOOL

JACK AND JILL WENT UP THE HILL

	White		X	721		776		I	3325
	318		−	722		782			3799
	334			725		817		*	3820
	351		/	727		838		B/S	725
	415		→	738		899		B/S	838
	435		\	758		987		B/S	987
	720		+	762		989		F/K	899

TWINKLE TWINKLE
LITTLE STAR

Special Days

Stitchers can always find the time to sew a card or gift for a special event such as a wedding, anniversary or new baby. This chapter is filled with delightful designs for such occasions, and many of the other designs in the book are ideal for cards, too. When it comes to displaying your card, there's a big range of styles and aperture shapes to choose from. If you cannot find exactly the card mount you want, try cutting your own from coloured card.

Wedding Day Champagne

Stitch a special band to go round a bottle of champagne as a gift for a couple who are getting married.

- ◆ **Aida band**
- ◆ **Graph paper and drawing equipment**
- ◆ **Velcro strip for fastening**
- ◆ **Sewing equipment**

DESIGN NOTES

I took the elements for my band from the charts on page 121, and arranged them horizontally.

MAKING THE BAND

1 Choose the correct size band for your design and cut it long enough to wrap around your bottle with an overlap.

2 Centre and stitch your design along the band. Leave enough unstitched band at each end for turning. Wrap the band around the bottle and mark the point where the ends overlap. Attach the Velcro strip in place.

Little Baby Band Sampler

Stitch a pretty band sampler to welcome a new baby using nursery motifs worked in pastel colours.

- ◆ **Aida band**
- ◆ **Felt for backing**
- ◆ **Decorative charms or buttons**
- ◆ **Graph paper and drawing equipment**
- ◆ **D ring for hanging**
- ◆ **Sewing equipment**

DESIGN NOTES

The elements for this vertical band sampler came from page 122. Turn to pages 6–9 for advice on how to chart your master design.

OPPOSITE: You will find plenty of designs suitable for a new baby card or gift among the charts on the following pages. I combined some of these motifs to make a delicate band sampler which I stitched on a yellow-edged aida band.

MAKING THE SAMPLER

1 Cut your aida band the correct size for your chart adding an extra 2.5 cm (1 in) for turnings. Start stitching about 14 aida blocks from the top of the band to allow for hemming, and leave the same amount of blocks unstitched at the other end.

2 Turn under about 7 aida blocks at each end of your completed band and press firmly in place. Attach any charms or buttons at this stage.

3 Use the aida band as a template to cut the backing felt making it about 6mm (¼ in) larger all round to frame your stitching. Stitch the D ring in place on the back of the felt before securing this to the aida. Then position and pin the wrong side of the aida band to the felt and slipstitch neatly along each edge.

Eighteenth Birthday Key

Make an original eighteenth-birthday gift by cutting a key from gold card and attaching a tag you have stitched with a red ribbon.

- ◆ **Perforated paper**
- ◆ **Ribbon**
- ◆ **Gold card**
- ◆ **Sharp scissors or craft knife**
- ◆ **Paper punch**

Draw the shape of your key on the gold card and cut out using a craft knife or sharp scissors. The design was stitched on perforated paper from the chart on page 124 and cut into the shape of a key tag. Punch a single hole at the top and thread a ribbon through it for attaching it to the gold card key.

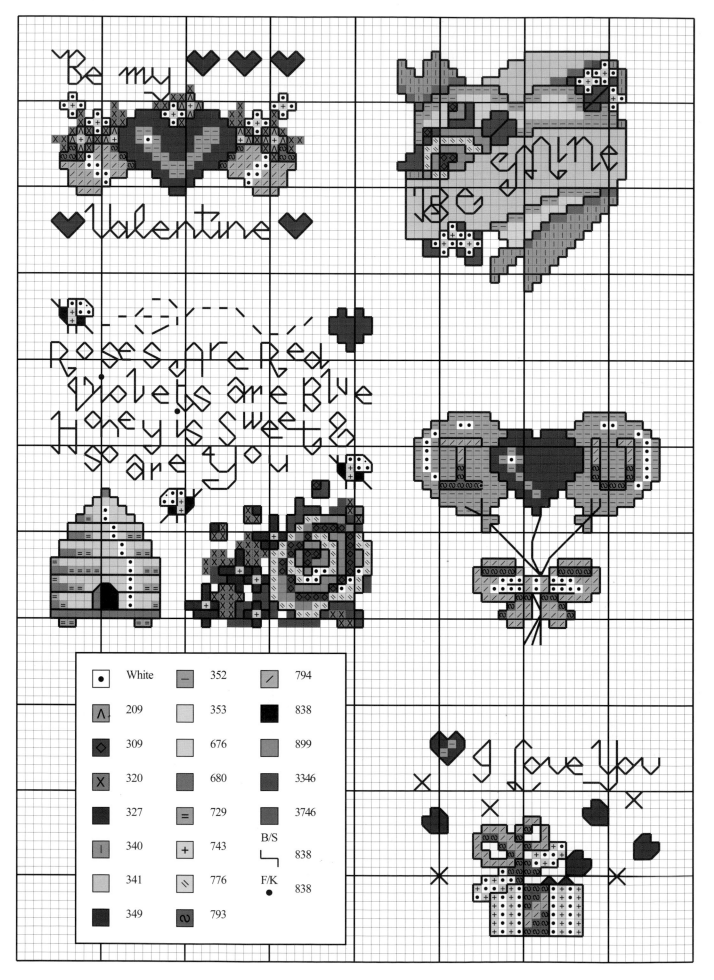

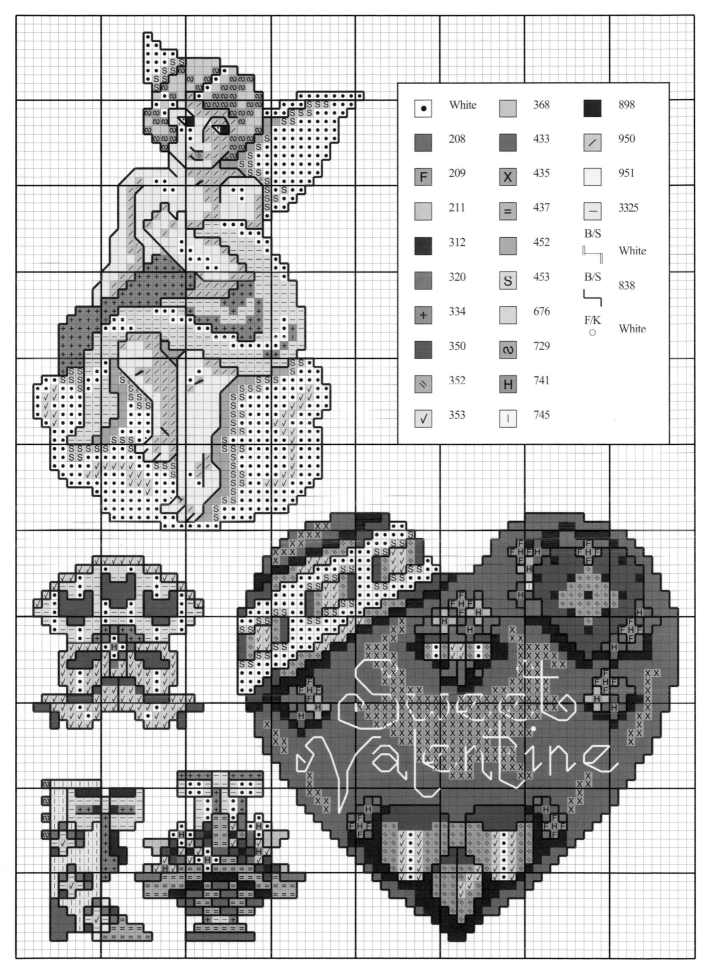

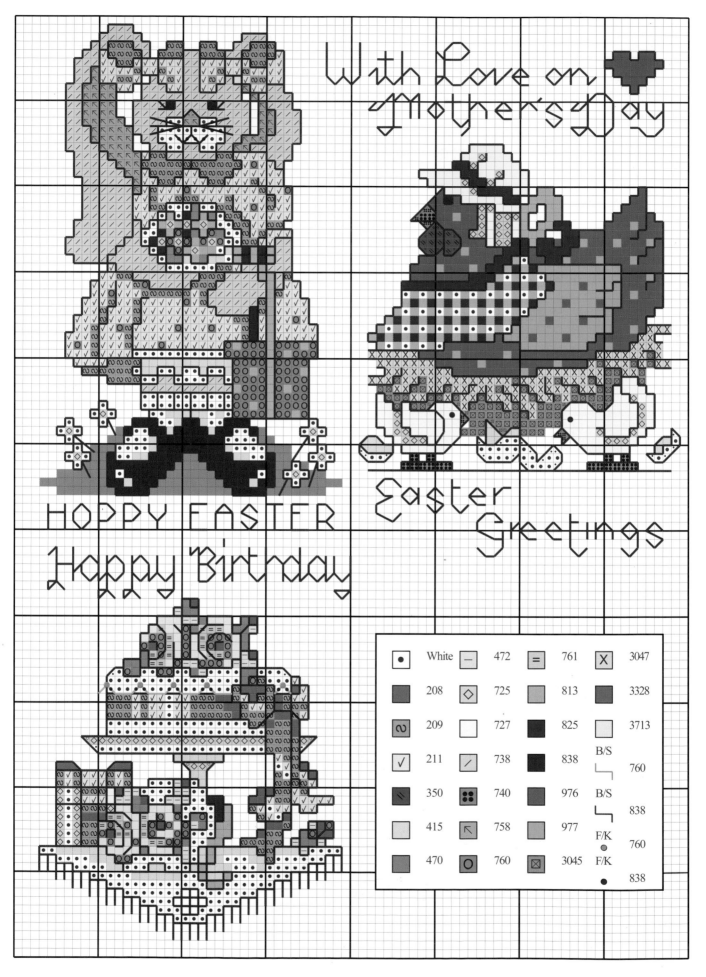

With Love on Mother's Day

HOPPY EASTER

Easter Greetings

Happy Birthday

●	White	—	472	=	761	X	3047
	208	◇	725		813		3328
2	209		727		825		3713
✓	211	/	738		838	B/S	760
	350	∷	740		976	B/S	838
	415	↖	758		977	F/K ●	760
	470	O	760	⊠	3045	F/K ●	838

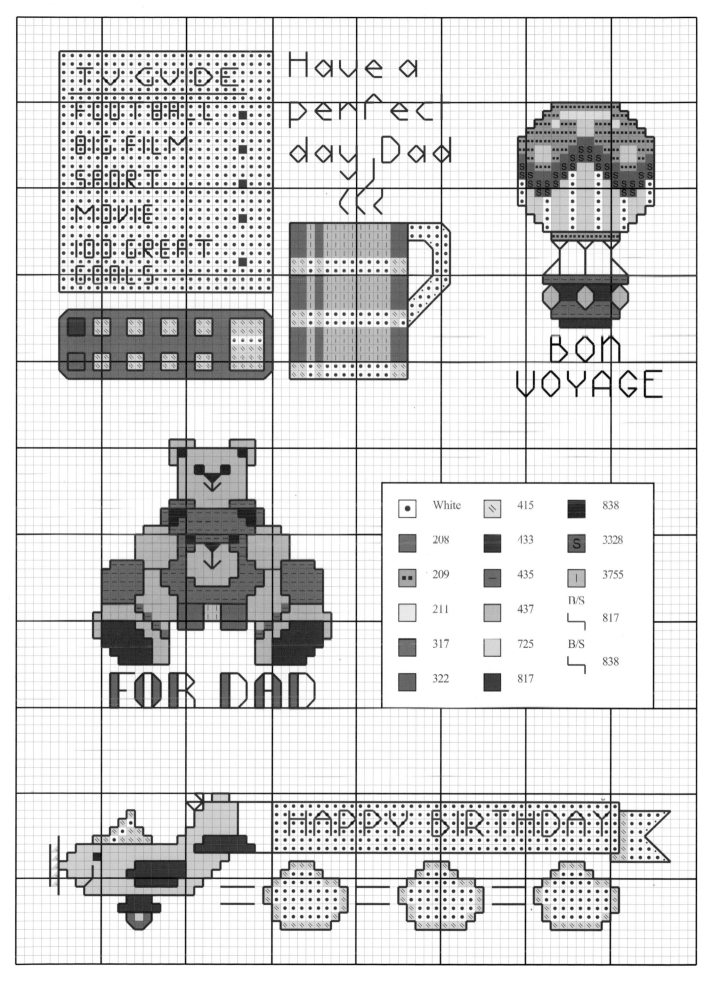

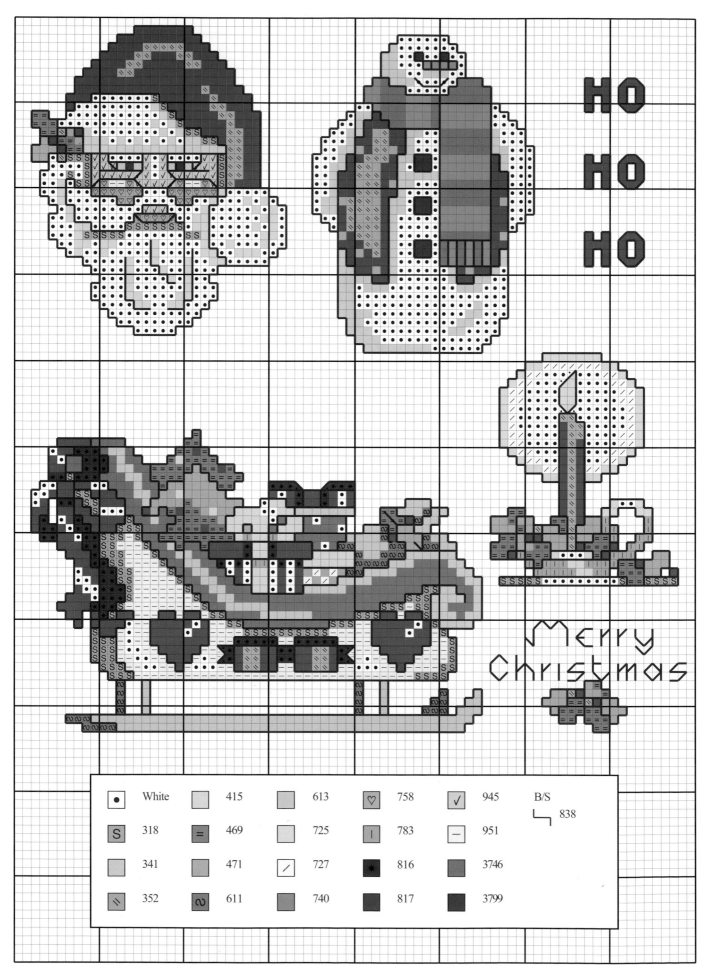

•	White		415		613	♡	758	✓	945	B/S	
S	318	=	469		725	|	783	—	951		838
	341		471	/	727	✱	816		3746		
\\\\	352	∽	611		740		817		3799		

HO

HO

HO

Merry Christmas

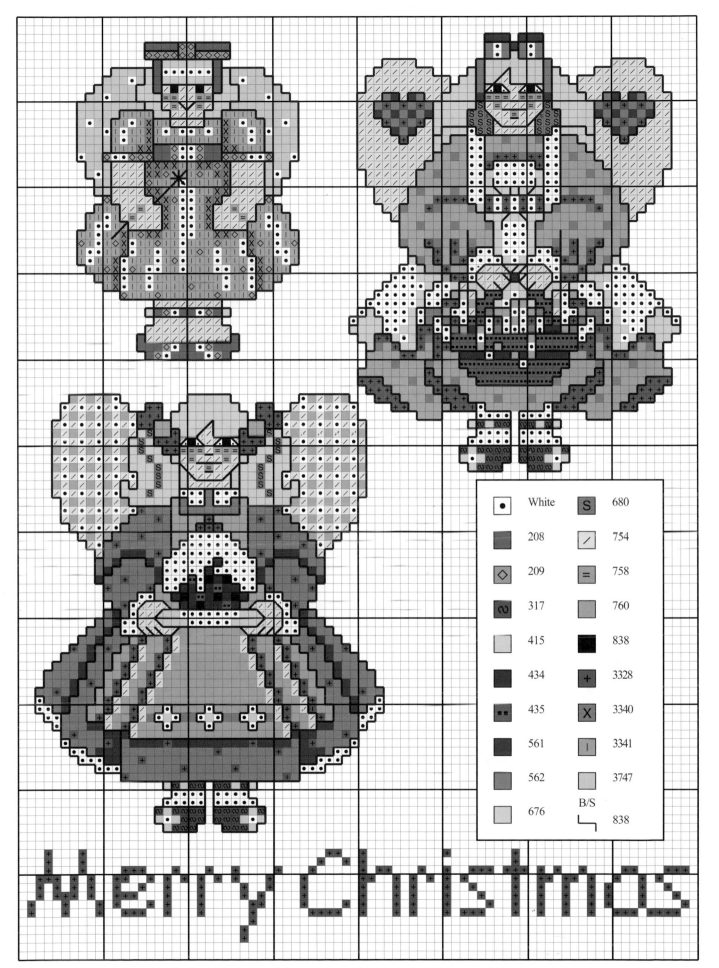

●	White	S	680
■	208	/	754
◇	209	=	758
ᘔ	317		760
	415	■	838
	434	+	3328
∷	435	X	3340
	561			3341
	562		3747
	676	B/S	
		└	838

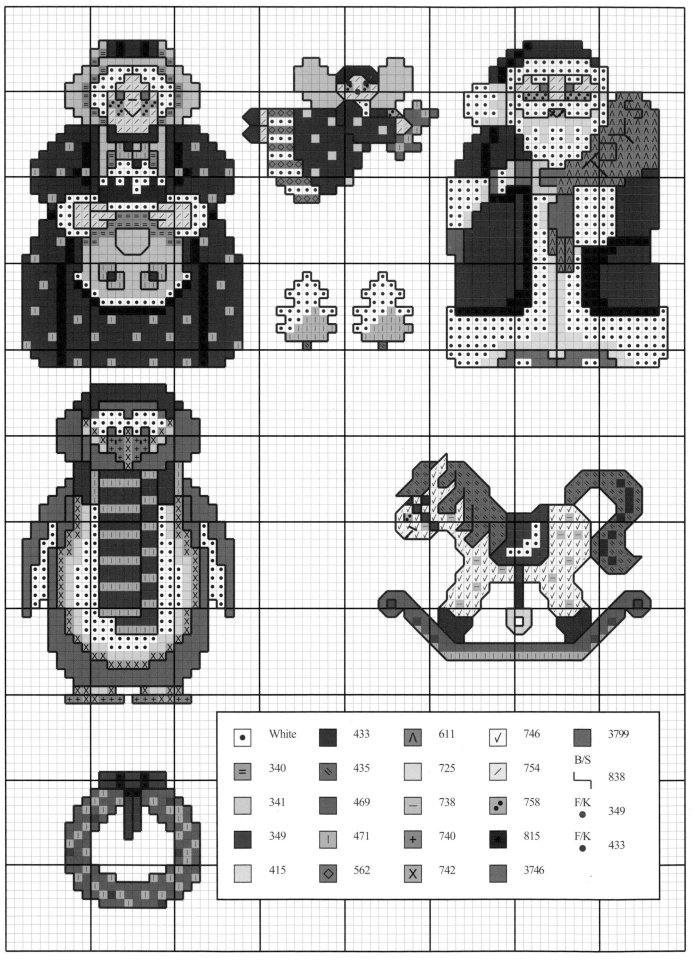

•	White	■	433	∧	611	√	746	■	3799
=	340	∖	435		725	/	754		B/S
	341		469	—	738	••	758	⌐	838
	349		471	+	740	✳	815	F/K •	349
	415	◇	562	X	742	■	3746	F/K •	433

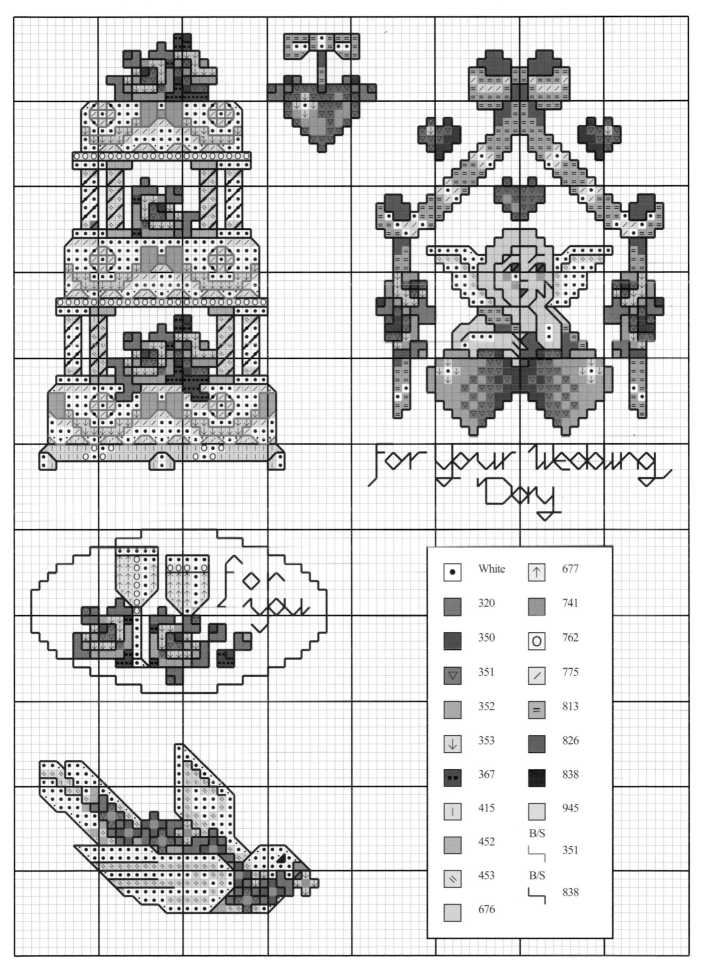

For your Wedding Day

●	White	↑	677
	320		741
	350	O	762
▽	351	/	775
	352	=	813
↓	353		826
∷	367		838
│	415		945
	452	B/S	351
╲	453	B/S	838
	676		

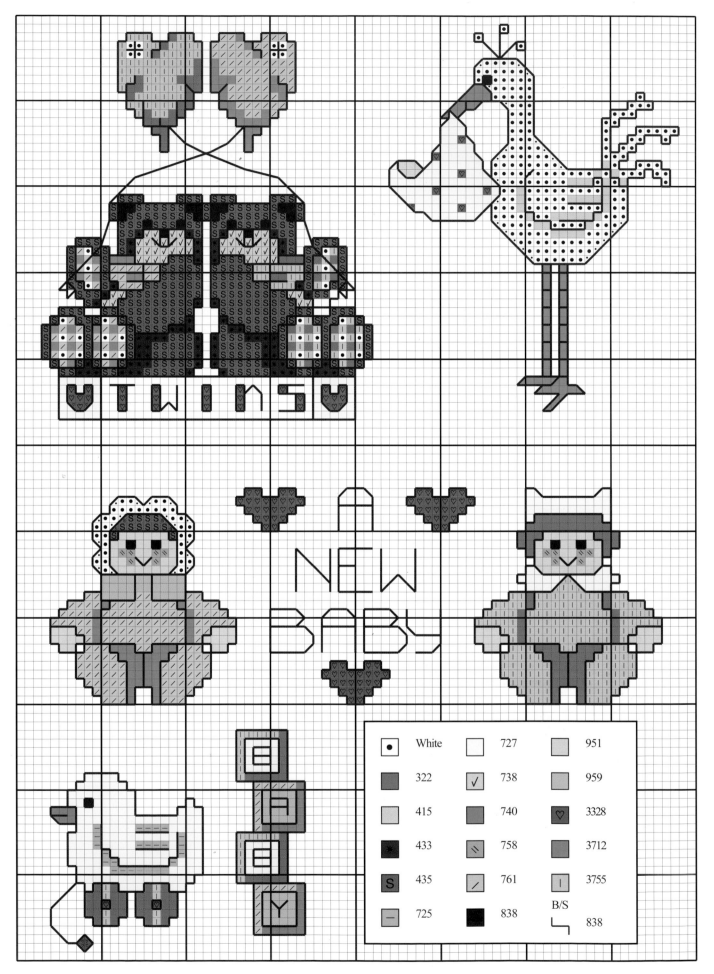

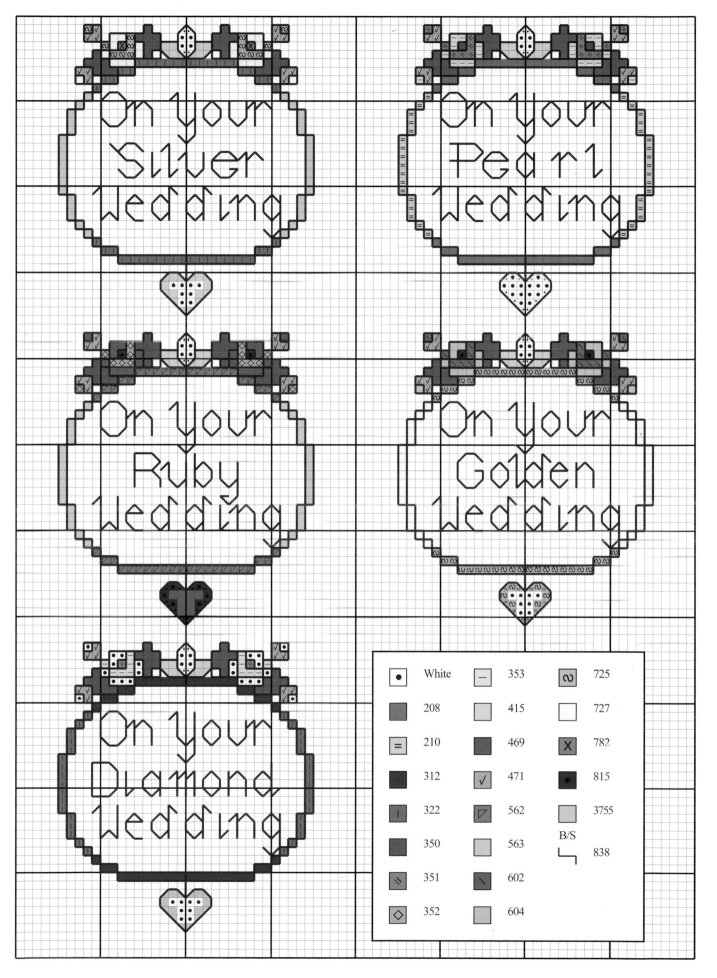

ABCDEFGHIJKLMN
OPQRSTUVWXYZ
abcdefghijklmn
opqrstuvwxyz &
123456789
0 1234567890 1234567890

ABCDEFGHIJKLMN
OPQRSTUVWXYZ
abcdefghijklmn pq
stuvwxyz

abcdefghijklmno
pqrstuvwxyz

	322
B/S	838

Acknowledgements

This book would never have been completed without the constant encouragement and patient love of my husband Ade. More than just my partner in life, he also spent many hours converting and checking all of these charts. As usual my mother, father, Andrew, Sarah and our daft dogs Anna and Dylan kept me going when I frequently felt like abandoning the whole project. Jennifer, Daphne, Varina and Chantal did a superb job in stitching the designs, tolerating my tight deadlines and scribbled instructions, and Pat Henson of the Crafty Stitcher then helped bring the projects to life with her expert framing that does so much to enhance my designs.

I must also extend my heartfelt thanks to Cheryl Brown and everyone at David & Charles for making every effort to help this book see the light of day. Thanks also go to my mother who helped make up most of the projects beautifully whilst doing my ironing and feeding us, and also to my dad who taught me to draw and kept me going with his 'team talks' when I needed encouragement. As always, my dearest friends Chris and Heather were there to laugh with me and listen to my moans. Last, and definitely least, our mate Stuart who cheers me up simply by being consistently more miserable and cynical than I am – now he's the only pharmacist to get a mention in a needlework book!

Amongst the people who were kind enough to supply materials for this book, I must, as always, thank Cara Ackerman at DMC for her continued and welcome support, Jo at Craft Creations, and Jacqui and Paul at Hantex who have an Aladdin's cave of goodies that helped inspire lots of these projects! The excellent computer software that made charting this book possible was supplied by IL-Soft of Oxford, whilst Rob Bracken of Bracken Software Ltd gave us his expert advice on setting up our new computer. And as ever I must also thank Juliet Bracken who skilfully edited this book and haunted my email in box again.

Suppliers

DMC Creative World Ltd
Pullman Road, Wigston, Leicestershire, LE18 2DY
Tel: 0116 281 104
Threads, fabric, afghan fabric, and baby bib.

Jacqui and Paul Smith, Hantex Ltd
Units 8–10, Lodge Farm Units, Wolverton Road,
Castlethorpe, Milton Keynes, MK19 7ES
Tel: 01908 511 331
Buttons, charms, Kunin felt, and wooden items.

Hobbycraft – Arts and Crafts Stores
Nationwide
A wide variety of craft supplies.

Craft Creations Ltd
Ingersoll House, Delamare Road, Cheshunt,
Herts, EN8 9HD
Tel: 01992 781900
Card blanks and specialist papers.

Index

Page numbers in *italic* indicate illustrations, and charts are indicated in **bold**